Strategic Management for Bankers

Richard W. Sapp
Portland State University

Roger W. Smith
Arthur Andersen & Co.

Published by Planning Executives Institute, Oxford, Ohio

ISBN 0-912841-19-2

Published by
Planning Executives Institute
5500 College Corner Pike
Oxford, Ohio 45056

TABLE OF CONTENTS

TABLE OF CONTENTS
(Continued)

TABLE OF CONTENTS
(Continued)

TABLE OF CONTENTS
(Continued)

ACKNOWLEDGEMENTS

The completion of any involved project requires the help and cooperation of many people. This Executive Series Monograph is no exception, but there are several individuals and groups of people to whom we are especially indebted. First, we gratefully acknowledge the financial support we received from the partners of Arthur Andersen & Co. and the faculty of the School of Business at Portland State University. In particular this includes Harry Demorest, Hank Laun and Richard Visse in Portland, Bob Kelley and Dave Nellemann in Chicago, and Charlie Balch in Atlanta. We also received notable aid from the following associates: Jack Wilborn, Verne Naito and Mark Avolio.

We are also grateful for the support received from Dean Martin A. Schatz and the faculty of the Roy E. Crummer Graduate School of Business at Rollins College in Winter Park, Florida. They provided the stimulating environment where much of this work was done.

We had the help of true professionals in putting this book together. The acute eye and sensitive pen of Janet Dow is present in many chapters. Michael Graybish and Chuck Vladika designed the cover and produced the graphics which so enhanced the value of this book. Also Pamela Gold and Marjorie Morford were very helpful in an editorial and clarification role. And much appreciation is due Jan Edwards who provided constant dedication and help in administering this effort.

We want to acknowledge the important contributions to the basic ideas in this book obtained in part from the writings of Michael Porter, George Steiner, Thomas Naylor, Jim Higgins, George Sawyer and Robert E. Seiler.

This monograph owes much to the editorial advice given by Henry Doofe and Jeff MacDonald of PEI. They recognized the need for such a book and initiated and supported its development. Henry reviewed the manuscript on several occasions for content and structure, as well as style. His comments were very helpful.

Although this book has benefited greatly from all this assistance the caveat must be added that any shortcomings and errors that may have occurred are solely ours.

* * *

Finally, and most importantly, our wives, Mary and Donna, deserve special mention. They exhibited extensive patience and provided the needed moral support that made this project possible. To them and our children, Coreen, Landry and Kendra, this book is dedicated.

Richard W. Sapp
Roger W. Smith

Portland, Oregon
January 1, 1984

BIOGRAPHICAL SKETCHES

Richard W. Sapp is an Associate Professor of Business at Portland State University. He has authored more than 15 articles in such professional journals as *The Magazine of Bank Administration, Managerial Planning* and *Management Accounting.* A frequent author on bank strategic planning, he has completed extensive research on the relationship between long-range planning and financial performance of U.S. commercial banks.

Dr. Sapp has a B.B.A. in finance from the University of Toledo and a M.S. and Ph. D. in accounting from the University of Houston. He has previously taught at the Roy E. Crummer Graduate School of Business and at the University of Houston. He is a Certified Public Accountant and a member of the Portland Chapter of PEI.

Roger W. Smith is a partner in the Portland office of Arthur Andersen & Co., an international public accounting and consulting firm. He holds degrees in management and engineering from Mississippi State University, and studied law and economics at the University of Virginia. He has also served as faculty and lead instructor of Arthur Andersen & Co.'s internal training program on strategic planning and strategic financial management.

Mr. Smith is currently treasurer and member of the national Board of Directors of the Planning Executives Institute. He is an active business and systems consultant within the Northwest banking community, a member of the Oregon Bankers Association and a member and active participant of his firm's Banking Industry Team.

1 OVERVIEW OF STRATEGIC MANAGEMENT

"Dig a well before you get thirsty."
... Chinese Proverb

Until recently, banking was generally profitable and experienced steady predictable growth. Bank assets were committed for relatively short periods, profits were stable and failures were rare. Additionally, competition was limited by federal, state and local agencies. Overall, the last 50 years has been a period of notable euphoria, when it was relatively difficult to lose money. Such is not the situation today.

The Current Situation

Professional bankers are facing a radically reshaped financial landscape, where there is much uncertainty about the future of small to medium-sized banks. Major regulatory changes have occurred and more are pending which will completely restructure the financial intermediary system. As a consequence, many experts in the banking industry are predicting by 1990 or sooner, the number of banks in the United States will drop from 14,000 to less than 10,000. Some are even predicting the figure will be much less than that. All agree by 1990 it will be a totally different industry.

The rate of change within the industry is staggering. Just in the last two years, we have witnessed more changes in the fundamental economic, regulatory, technological and social forces affecting banks than in any time since the Depression. Factors such as double-digit inflation, recession, foreign debts, intense competition, new financial products and services, revised pricing strategies and deregulation have completely reshaped the financial services industry. Not since the 1930s have bankers had to so quickly and radically alter their thinking. No longer can one rely on the traditional pillars of an exclusive product and market, a protected geographic franchise and ceilings on interest paid depositors. There is no assurance of survival.

The prosperous days of limited entry, courteous competition and statutory protection have fostered generations of bankers who are not accustomed to the risks and rewards they are facing today. Unfortunately, many are not equipped for the intensity and diversity of the new competition and they will not survive. Instead, the rewards of success will go to those bankers who can manage the complexities of the modern financial institution, cope with the dynamic environmental forces and deal with competition from firms that were not even part of their industry a few years ago.

Let's take stock for a moment of the most likely situation for the 1980s:

- Competition for funds and customers will become even more intense.
- Profits will be squeezed through shrinking spreads and increasing operating costs.
- Automation will accelerate at an even faster pace.
- More regulatory changes will occur.
- Bank customer contact locations will grow nationally and internationally.
- Retail customer demands will stress convenience, price and services.
- Smaller banks, unable to compete on price, will increasingly seek to establish an industry niche which differentiates them in the eyes of their customers.
- Banks will have more difficulty finding and developing qualified managers and staff.
- Competition from non-bank institutions like Shearson/American Express, Merrill Lynch and Sears will continue to cause a redefinition of financial services.
- Limited opportunities to raise external capital will put even greater pressure on short-term profits.
- The image of community banks as full-service financial in-

stitutions will be in jeopardy as low-cost producers like Citicorp and Bank of America move into their markets.

In this environment of industry shakeout, some doom-and-gloomers say there is no hope, particularly for the small to medium-sized bank. They would have you believe that the only banks that can successfully weather this revolution are the large money-center, high-volume, low-cost institutions which can attract capital and afford the necessary technology. We disagree!

We believe the future is still good for banking. There are profitable opportunities for every bank, regardless of its size. For example, the small to medium-sized bank, which some would have you believe cannot compete against the giants, has some competitive advantages:

- The convenience of the bank's location.
- Personal contact and services offered along with a meaningful customer relationship developed over the years.
- Relative flexibility in adapting to changing market needs.

The professional banker cannot, however, count on selected competitive advantages alone. To survive he[1] must also:

- Be innovative.
- Cost and price bank products and services.
- Manage interest rate risk effectively.
- Attract and reward bright ambitious people.
- Market the bank's products to the appropriate segments of the community.
- Develop, formulate and implement intelligent strategy.
- Think.

---

[1]Masculine pronouns are used throughout this monograph instead of an awkward he and/or she convention.

How does a banker go about positioning his bank so it is not only one of the survivors, but a profitable success? The purpose of this monograph is to answer that question. We have presented an effective methodology called STRATEGIC MANAGEMENT to aid bankers in successfully dealing with the pressure and opportunities of their new industry.

What Is Strategic Management?

As consultants, we have determined that the most important criteria of bank effectiveness is not its operational efficiency but its ability to adapt to environmental change. Strategic management is both a process and a philosophy for determining and controlling the bank's relationship to its changing environment. As a process, it defines approaches and techniques to help bank management adapt to the dynamics of today's financial industry. Through the use of objectives and strategies, strategic management endeavors to achieve efficient programs to accomplish the bank's mission. As a philosophy, strategic management changes how managers look at competition, customers, markets and even the bank itself. Its purpose is to stimulate management's awareness of the strategic implications of environmental events and internal decisions.

Strategic management provides a fresh approach to re-emphasizing responsibilities managers have always had. This approach has been necessitated by the rapid redefinition of the entire financial industry. Properly implemented, strategic management permeates all major activities and decision making by raising the level of consciousness and providing valuable insights that are otherwise unobtainable. Overall, strategic management is the best fully integrated approach we know of for managing change.

Effective strategic management is characterized by:

- Clear direction and purpose.
- Objectives, goals and strategies consistent with the business mission.
- Continuous monitoring of internal and external environments.
- Integration of operating budgets and profit plans with the strategic plan.

- Continuous monitoring of progress with revision of plans and programs as appropriate.

- Creation of a strategic atmosphere that fosters a team spirit.

- Commitment of necessary resources and the development of systems to provide necessary management information.

The resources and effort required to develop a strategic management philosophy in many banks could be quite significant. It is a major commitment which should not be undertaken lightly. Thoughtful consideration is given not only to the financial requirements, but particularly to the demands placed upon the bank's personnel. It will require training and educating bank managers to the new way of making decisions. And, it most certainly will require that some changes take place in the existing order of things.

The costs, as material as they could be, must be weighted against the benefits we have observed in our client banks. These benefits from strategic management include:

- Recognition of potential strategic implications of every major action and event.

- Better understanding of the bank and its industry.

- More effective decision making.

- Improved objectives, goals and strategies.

- Reduced resistance to change through proper implementation.

- Enhanced communications and mutual understandings.

Strategic Planning Pyramid

To realize the full benefits of strategic management, the bank must blend together three seemingly distinct elements into an integrated process. These elements are:

- **Strategic planning**—Strategic planning is the core of strategic management. It refers to the process of formulating the bank's mission, objectives and goals and developing strategies to achieve them. Strategic planning creates a conceptual framework that incorporates the external environment, characterized by risk, change and uncertainty, into the bank's long-term decisions.

- **Strategic action**—Strategic action is the implementation phase of strategic management. It refers to managing the implementation of the strategic plan and translating the strategies into actions. This requires linking the longer term strategies to the shorter term measures like budgets and motivating individuals to accomplish them.

- **Strategic thinking**—Strategic thinking represents an integration of strategic planning and strategic action. We believe strategic thinking must be achieved before any bank can complete the evolutionary process needed for a sound strategic management system.

We have used a pyramid (Figure 1-1) as the graphic medium to show how these three elements are related. The reasons for choosing a three-dimensional figure are that each face touches every other face and each face depends on other faces for stability. This most closely portrays how we envision strategic management. We see it as a process that has height, depth and breadth with a high degree of interdependence between its elements.

Strategic Management Model

The chapters of this monograph are organized around the planning, action and thinking framework we just illustrated. Figure 1-2 shows how each chapter relates to this framework.

As noted on the Strategic Management Model, the first phase, "Strategic Planning," is broken down into six major topics and examined in Chapters 2 through 7. The next phase of strategic management is "Strategic Action," which concentrates on implementation and monitoring the strategic plan. This phase is discussed in Chapters 8 through 11. The last phase, "Strategic Thinking," effectively integrates the plan into daily decision making. This concept is explored in Chapters 12 through 14.

Although the size of each "slice of the pie" appears equal, this is not meant to imply that the same level of effort or resources are re-

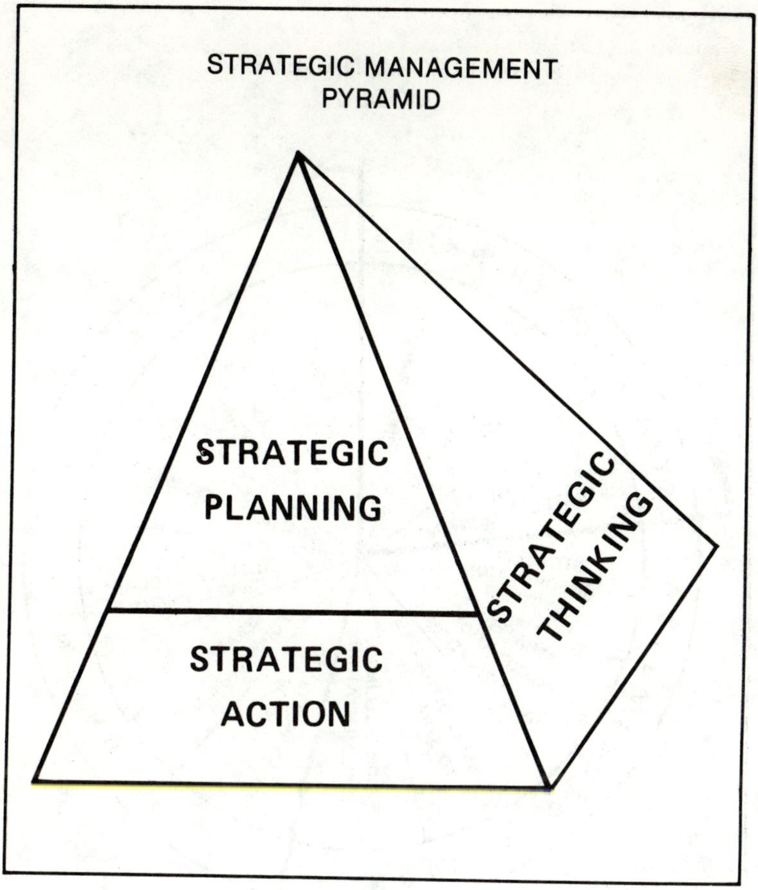

FIGURE 1-1

quired for each step in the overall process. The actual effort necessary depends upon bank size and sophistication, the results of past efforts, the capabilities of management, and the unique competitive situation facing the individual bank.

Strategic vs. Other Types of Planning

From our discussions with bank executives, we have noted that some confusion exists surrounding the use of the term "strategic planning." This has been the result of its widespread use by managers to encompass such activities as annual budgeting, operating and profit planning, and tactical programming. For this reason, it might be well to differentiate strategic planning from

STRATEGIC MANAGEMENT MODEL

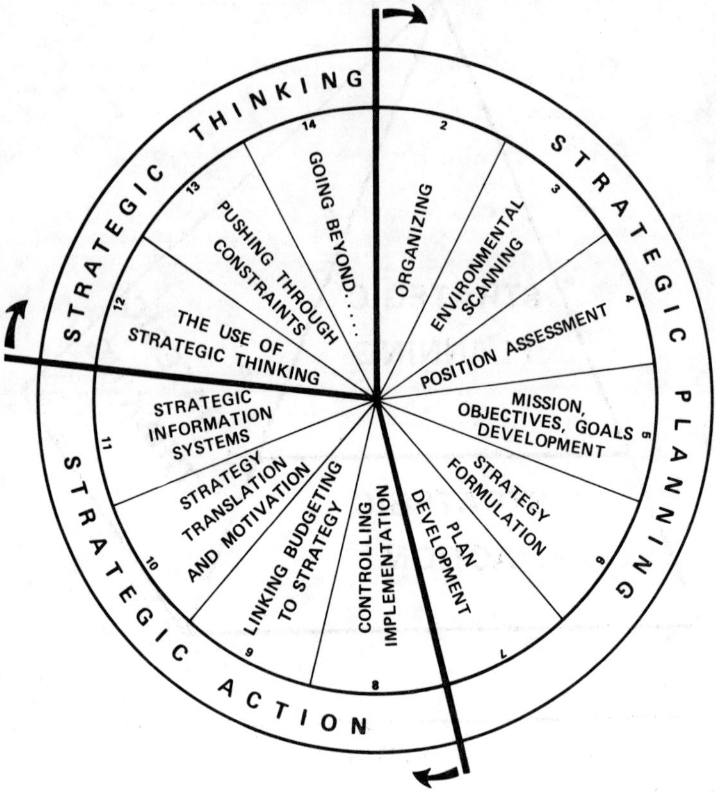

FIGURE 1-2

other forms of planning. Figure 1-3 enumerates the more commonly used planning terms and offers a definition and selected contrasting characteristics of each.

The principal attributes differentiating strategic planning include:

- Assessing the *future impact* of current decisions.

- Providing a *structure* for dealing with *risk and uncertainty.*

- Considering *alternative courses of action* in response to changing environmental situations.

- Incorporating a *process* for determining the bank's purpose, direction, and expected results.

TYPES OF PLANNING

Type	Definition	Characteristics
Annual	Represents the specific goals and action programs for the current year of the strategic plan.	• Quantitive benchmarks for short-term performance • Prepared by organizational unit • One year time horizon • Monthly detail compared to actual results
Financial	A financial and narrative expression of expected results.	• Explicit statement of goals • Accounting orientation • Cash flow and cash budgets • Financial statement presentation
Functional or Operational	Process of determining specific functional objectives, goals and strategies based on overall corporate plan.	• Major areas include marketing, financial, human resources, information processing • Typically 1-3 years planning horizon • Could link annual planning to strategic planning
Tactical	Task oriented planning to deploy resources to accomplish one or more specific short-term objectives.	• Detailed view of activities • Describe how specific strategies are achieved • Typically one year horizon
Long Range	Financial extrapolation of short-term financial plan for a long-term horizon.	• Very stable industries • Typically 5-20 year horizon • Corporate orientation • Formalized
Strategic	A framework for managers to enable them to make decisions which affect the future in an environment of risk and uncertainty.	• Long-term horizon • High degree of environmental uncertainty • Creative • Less detail

FIGURE 1-3

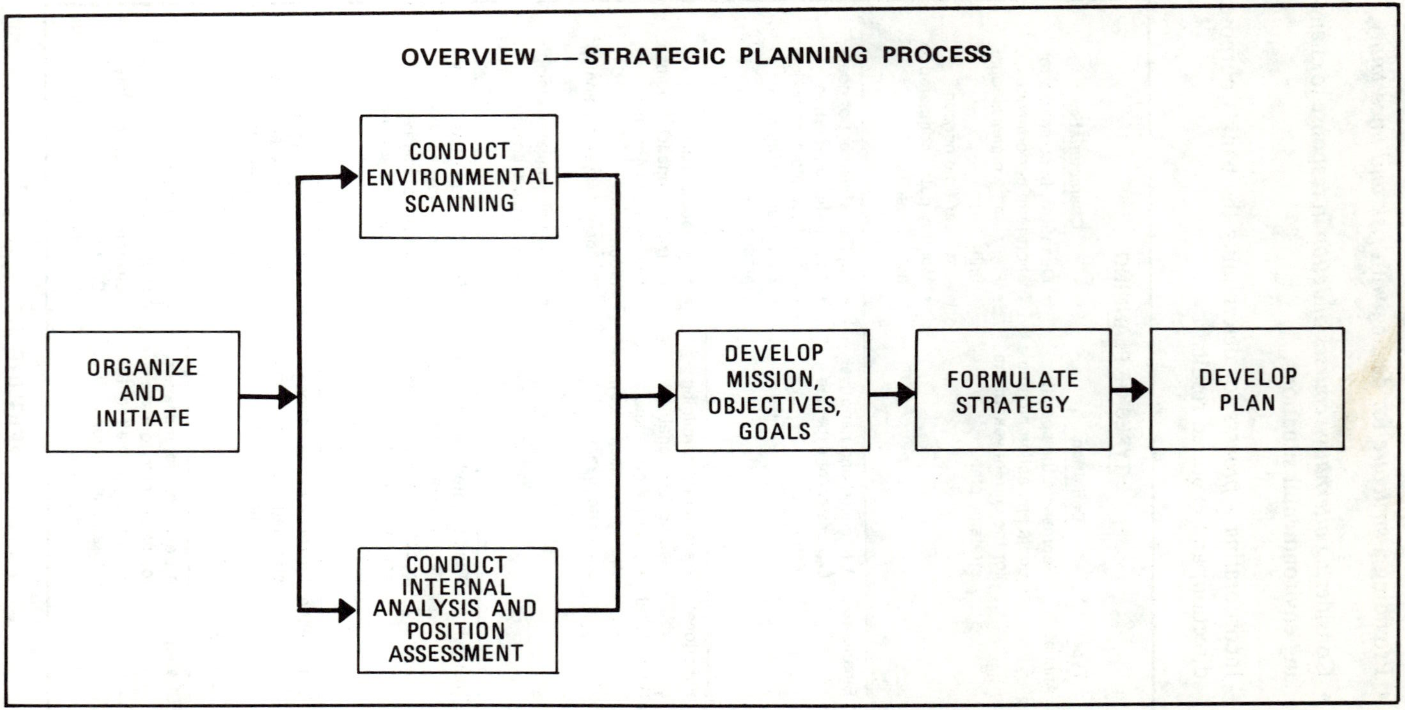
OVERVIEW — STRATEGIC PLANNING PROCESS
ORGANIZE AND INITIATE
CONDUCT ENVIRONMENTAL SCANNING
CONDUCT INTERNAL ANALYSIS AND POSITION ASSESSMENT
DEVELOP MISSION, OBJECTIVES, GOALS
FORMULATE STRATEGY
DEVELOP PLAN

FIGURE 1-4

Strategic Planning Process

Our approach to strategic planning is illustrated in Figure 1-4. The process is a series of steps beginning with organizing and initiating. The major activities in a strategic plan are:

- Environmental scanning.
- Internal analysis and position assessment.
- Developing mission, objectives and goals.
- Formulating strategy.
- Developing the plan.

In the strategic planning portion of this monograph, we will be using flowcharts expanding upon the one illustrated in Figure 1-4.

The flowcharts allow us to simplify a complex process by breaking it up into understandable tasks. Because strategic planning is a repetitive process with numerous "feedback loops," we have taken this approach to simplify its presentation.

* * *

We recognize the tremendous uncertainty bankers face each day and we offer this monograph as a means of providing you with some practical assistance. We have tried to keep things simple and to present our ideas in a step-by-step, logical manner. We begin in Chapter 2 with Organizing and Initiating Strategic Planning.

STRATEGIC PLANNING

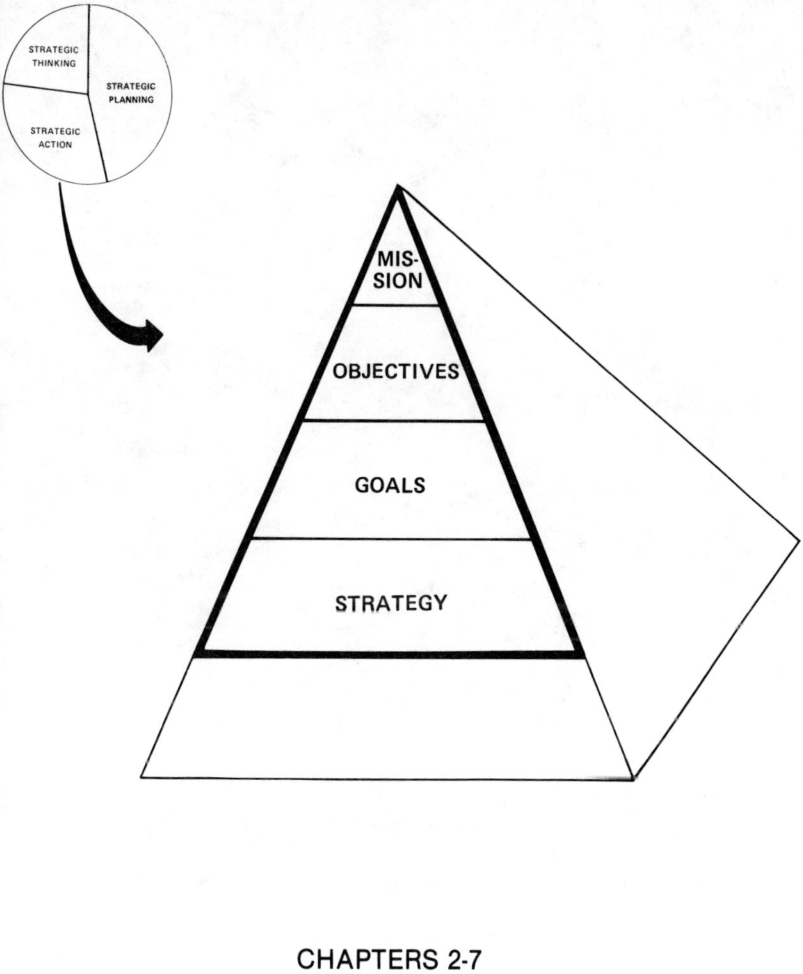

CHAPTERS 2-7

2 ORGANIZING AND INITIATING STRATEGIC PLANNING

"There is nothing more difficult to take in hand, more perilous to conduct, or more uncertain in the success, than to take the lead in the introduction of a new order of things."

... Machiavelli

We all read and hear much about the virtues of strategic planning. We are told that such a plan will help you as a banker cope with future uncertainties in an organized and systematic manner. We are bombarded with numerous seminar offerings on the subject.

Although these presentations emphasize the importance of such planning, the specifics of how to initiate strategic planning are often missing. The banker is then left with little to guide him. For example, he needs to know how to create an effective planning climate, how to establish and communicate top management's support of strategic planning, how to organize the project and its participants, and how to actually begin. In this chapter we will discuss these important matters.

Creating the Desired Planning Climate

Over the years we have observed and consulted numerous banks and other businesses as they developed strategic plans. We learned from our work that the success of a strategic plan depends as much on the planning climate as it does on the techniques used to develop the plan.

We have observed bank planning climates where employees have a strong fear of failure and management has a "no room for error" attitude. In this kind of climate, there is more concern with timely completion of preprinted planning forms than with the substance of the plan. Creativity is stifled and little, if any, real planning is accomplished. In contrast, we have been in banks where you could feel the "can do" spirit. The employees are market-oriented and the management team is ready to respond to any challenges. This is clearly the desired planning environment.

An important attribute of an effective climate is an accepted, demonstrated belief on the part of bank personnel that strategic planning is a valuable, significant activity. It is the accepted way of life in the bank and it permeates management's daily activities and attitudes. A strategic plan is much easier to develop in such a positive atmosphere.

Although we agree that establishing a desired climate is necessary, it is not easy to do or quickly accomplished. Typically employees feel threatened by change and may be slow to adopt a new approach to a familiar task. In fact, we find it generally takes several years for this positive attitude toward planning to permeate a bank. We would be unrealistic to expect an immediate, enthusiastic acceptance of strategic planning from every bank employee. They may be skeptical at first. They may feel this is another number-crunching, form-filling, meeting-ladened exercise, that will soon find its way to the CEO's back shelf to gather dust and be gratefully forgotten.

On the other hand, if appropriate initial steps are taken and a sustained commitment shown by senior management, it is a reasonable expectation that strategic planning — and eventually strategic thinking — will become a way of life in the bank. The next section overviews how to organize and initiate strategic planning to create a positive planning climate.

Overview of Planning-to-Plan

We illustrate our approach to the organizing and initiating phase of strategic planning in Figure 2-1.Tasks called for include:

- Establish top management support, a critical first step in creating the desired planning environment.
- Develop preliminary mission, objectives and goals for the bank and prepare a set of common economic assumptions for use throughout the bank.
- Define the planning units around which the strategic plan will be built.

- Designate planning roles and responsibilities of individuals who will be involved in developing the strategic plan.

- Develop work programs and a completion timetable.

- Identify preliminary data requirements and initiate data collection efforts.

- Communicate the planning process and guidelines to employees.

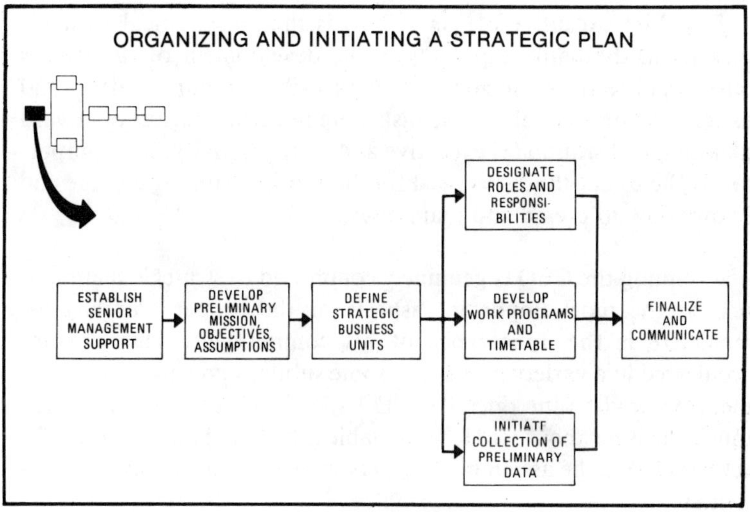

FIGURE 2-1

The essence of the organizing and initiating phase is to develop a "plan for planning." This plan should be written and along with related material, be incorporated into a planning manual. A properly constructed planning manual will be an important tool for instructing and communicating within the bank on their future planning activities.

Establishing Senior Management Support

We will define senior management in a small to medium-sized bank as the president and chief executive officer, the chairman and other key members of the board of directors, and members of the executive committee. The support and involvement of this group throughout the strategic planning, strategic action and strategic thinking phases is critical if a realistic business plan is to be developed and implemented.

Without this group's support and involvement, the whole effort will flounder. Under those circumstances the best plan one could hope for would be just an extension of past results. Such a plan would be devoid of strategic thinking or creative strategies.

Chief Executive Officer

The chief executive officer (CEO) is the most critical strategic planner in the bank, especially in the development of the bank's mission, objectives and goals. He organizes the planning effort and assigns the best people to the tasks. He nourishes attitudes toward planning and stimulates executive and staff creativity. Most importantly, he understands the need for the proper planning climate and knows how to create and maintain it.

Assuming the CEO is genuinely committed to strategic planning, one of the most important aspects of the proper planning atmosphere is the appearance of his commitment. This is communicated in a variety of ways — some subtle, some not. For example, how much time does the CEO spend on planning? How enthusiastic is he about it? How available is he to the participating executives? Does he assign his best personnel to strategic planning activities?

Employees will learn much about his attitude by simple observation. They know the CEO's time is valuable and cannot be wasted. Thus, the time he allocates to this project will be a strong indicator of his commitment. His participation will be closely watched. Evidence that his commitment is an illusion will surely sabotage further efforts. For example, if the CEO delegates the *total* process to the planning officer, he is in effect stating that the project does not merit his time and attention. That unspoken declaration will be picked up by employees just as if it were announced over the public address system. No matter the number of memos, meetings or speeches about the value of strategic planning, if others believe the CEO is not committed to it, the effort will fail.

On the other hand, the rewards of strategic planning will also be lost if the CEO makes the decisions single-handedly. A strong-willed CEO could inhibit the whole planning process unless he clearly delegates authority and responsibility for the *details* of strategy development to his managers and the executive planning committee. Such delegation provides many opportunities for the managers to contribute to the bank's strategic position.

Thus, the chief executive officer has a critically important position in the planning process.

Important roles of the CEO are:

- Establish the bank's mission.
- Appoint an executive planning committee.
- Establish preliminary bank-wide objectives.
- Act as liaison to the board of directors.
- Commit needed time and resources to the project.
- Act as the strategic planning catalyst.
- Monitor progress and recognize achievement.
- Maintain a high-level bank-wide perspective while avoiding excessive detail.

Board of Directors

Historically, the board chairman and directors in most smaller banks have had limited association with the process of developing a strategic plan. Although commonly they reviewed and approved whatever effort was made, they had little input in the formation of mission, objectives, goals and strategies.

But all that has changed. After the financial collapse of several major financial institutions, the role of the board has been examined more closely. We believe the board can expect greater involvement in the strategic decision-making process. In fact, the FDIC has mandated this board involvement. The days of "rubber stamp" boards are gone.

We believe the directors should act as a sounding board for the planning process as the mission statement, objectives, goals and strategies are developed. Board members are in a unique position to take a broad, bankwide, fully integrated view of the plan. This is often difficult for those involved on a daily basis with plan details. The board can provide an external view on whether the strategic plan is realistic or not.

The board's acknowledged support of the strategic planning process is critical for the CEO. Without their support the credibility of top management's commitment to the plan is questionable. Thus, the board also plays a significant role in creating the desired planning climate.

Executive Planning Committee

The executive planning committee has significant involvement in all phases of the planning process. Their most important roles, however, are to provide overall direction to the planning process and to coordinate the CEO's broad perspective with the more detailed strategic plan.

The planning committee translates the CEO's mission and objectives into requirements appropriate for the bank's various units. They are also responsible for approving the planning process developed by the planning officer, reviewing material, monitoring plan progress and reporting to the CEO. Other committee duties are:

- Establishing planning policies.
- Reviewing environmental assumptions and forecasts.
- Assessing the bank's internal strengths, weaknesses, and the environmental opportunities and threats.
- Reviewing objectives, goals and strategies.
- Coordinating with outside consultants.
- Reviewing planning resource allocation.
- Reviewing planning priorities.

• Establishing standards to measure accomplishment.

In small to medium-sized banks, the existing executive committee is often designated as the executive planning committee. The membership typically includes: the CEO, the executive vice president, vice presidents from each unit (e.g., commercial, retail, trust, etc.) and the heads of functional departments (e.g., branch operations, legal, data processing, administration, etc.). The committee membership should reflect the bank's needs and talent.

After the planning process is completed, the goal of this committee is to meet regularly throughout the year to discuss strategy and strategy development. Using the existing executive committee as the planning committee can weaken the strategic planning process if the committee discusses nonstrategy issues when the focus should be on the bank strategy. These discussions, while appropriate for the executive committee meetings are not appropriate for the planning committee. We have found it helpful to slightly realign the planning committee membership to differentiate it from the executive committee by including other key managers or possibly an outside consultant. This realignment helps reinforce the committee's purpose and direction.

Preliminary Mission, Objectives and Assumptions

At the onset of planning, the CEO, board of directors and the executive planning committee must agree on the following:

- Preliminary mission
- Tentative bank objectives
- Initial set of economic assumptions

We say *preliminary, tentative* and *initial* because we expect the mission, objectives and assumptions will be revised throughout the planning process. These serve only as starting points to guide the planning committee and bank managers until the formal mission, objectives and goals can be developed. This preliminary work is basically top management's "going-in" position on certain strategic issues.

The triangular face of the Strategic Management Pyramid, introduced in Chapter 1, is portrayed in Figure 2-2. It illustrates the hierarchial nature of mission, objectives, goals and strategies. We will use this triangle as our framework for discussing the major components needed to develop the base of the triangle, that is, realistic achievable strategies.

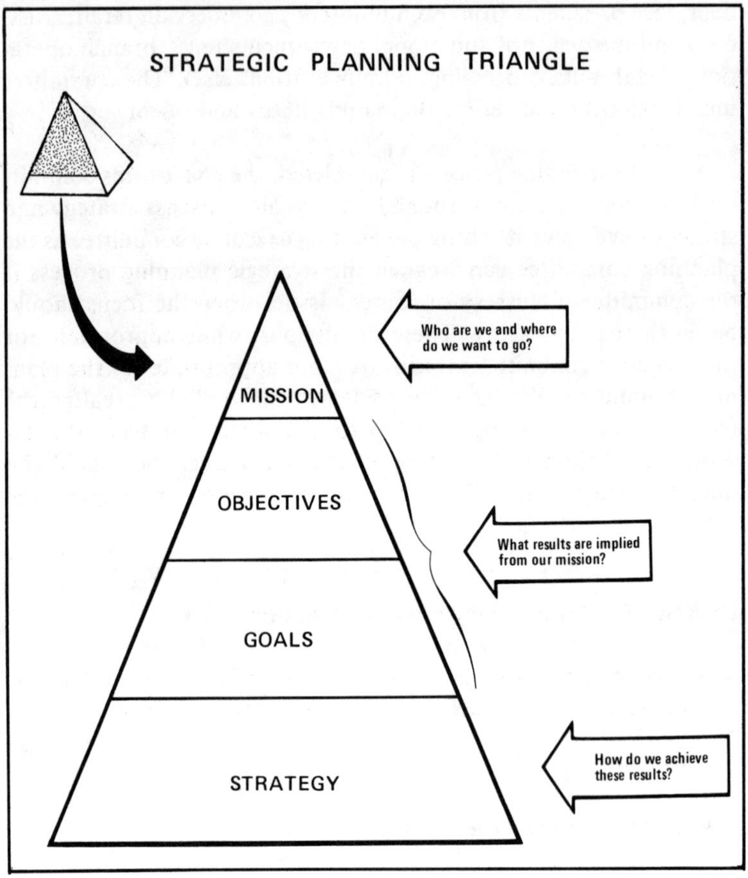

FIGURE 2-2

Preliminary Mission

The mission statement gives the CEO the opportunity to communicate his ideas on the bank's future. He can state the purpose of the bank and describe its distinguishing characteristics. The statement is the starting point for the whole planning process.

The preliminary mission is the CEO's position as the planning process begins. He has defined the role the bank will play in the new competitive market and identified his ideas on the scope of the bank operations, services and markets. He may have even redefined the historical mission of the bank.

A redefinition of purpose has become increasingly important in today's marketplace. For example, Sears, Roebuck & Co., historically one of the nation's top retailers recently changed their strategy dramatically. Sears was having difficulty increasing growth in retail sales and decided to embark on a daring new strategy in later 1981. The company sought to remain the top retailer *and* become the country's No. 1 financial institution by moving into consumer financial services. In order to achieve this goal, it moved into the brokerage business, real estate and money-market funds. These businesses will be added to their existing financial services — a full range of insurance products, savings and loan operations, loans, commercial realty and store leasing.

Sears has both the means to enter these new markets and, most importantly, the necessary distribution network. During its strategic planning, Sears recognized its strength of well-established distribution channels and decided to use these channels to market consumer financial services. The company continues to see itself as a retail business offering a wide spectrum of products. Bankers now realize Sears will become a major competitor as the retailing giant incorporates in-store ATMs and acquires deposit-taking institutions outside of California.

After becoming victims of "diagonal integration" in the financial services market, some larger banks have redefined their purpose to become the aggressor. Several banks have begun attacking the insurance industry. Just as Sears believed their distribution network provided a strategic advantage for entering the banking industry, bankers now believe their branch network offers strategic opportunity to sell insurance.

First Interstate Bancorp, for example, with approximately 1,000 branches and an average of 300,000 customers each day is interested in the insurance business. Their distribution system and larger customer base might keep start-up costs low and be more cost effective than the existing insurance agency network. Citicorp and Security Pacific also have an interest in insurance. Both are trying to qualify under recent South Dakota legislation circumventing federal regulations of "non-banking" activities such as insurance sales.

Failure to contemplate a redefinition of purpose could put constraints on the bank's strategic planning. You must always keep your mind open during the development of your preliminary mission and look for ways to capitalize on your competitive strengths and market opportunities.

Since this mission is preliminary, you should expect to revise it as you learn about the external environment and gain a better understanding of your own situation. Figure 2-3 illustrates one institution's preliminary mission statement.

PRELIMINARY MISSION STATEMENT
MOUNTAIN VIEW NATIONAL BANK OF COLORADO

The primary responsibility of Mountain View National Bank of Colorado is to maximize the economic value of the Bank for its stockholders. This will be accomplished by identifying and serving all legitimate financial needs of this market area in order to generate an above-average return on assets within an environment of exceptional customer service. Mountain View National will optimize this long run return to stockholders by building a banking and financial services institution more responsive than its competitors to the needs of the central Colorado Rockies. The Bank explicitly recognizes that its capacity to optimize stockholder return depends on the commitment of its employees. Mountain View National holds that its purpose includes maximizing the opportunities of employees to benefit by their association with the Bank.

MVNB's primary markets are the households and the small to medium sized businesses within its service area. To these markets the Bank will bring a select line of wholesale and retail banking services each justified by its contribution to the Bank's profitability.

Knowledgeable of its community, MVNB will anticipate the financial needs of its customers and create new opportunities "to put the area's resources to work locally."

MVNB's function are (1) to support the businesses which operate in and reinvest in its service area and (2) to share with the community the good judgement and business perspectives of its officers and employees.

FIGURE 2-3

Preliminary Objectives

From the preliminary mission statement, the CEO and the executive planning committee derive preliminary objectives. These objectives identify the results that were broadly stated in the preliminary mission statement. Developing objectives is the first step in translating the mission into actions. For example, a segment of the bank's mission might be:

> The primary mission of the Great Western Bank is to maximize the long-term value of the Bank to its owners.

From this mission, several objectives could be developed, for example:

- Improve the quality of management and employee skills.
- Strengthen and reorganize the loan department.
- Develop a capability to provide brokerage services.
- Establish a more competitive trust operation to support bank growth.

Areas commonly covered by preliminary objectives include:

- Profitability
- Growth
- Market share
- Services mix
- Operations
- Facilities
- Personnel levels
- Capital requirements
- Marketing
- Image
- Technology
- Stakeholder relations

Preliminary Goals

Some banks find it valuable to translate preliminary objectives into preliminary goals. Principal characteristics of goals are:

- Specific
- Quantified
- Dated

Goals express in *specific* terms what the objectives state in general terms. For example, in the prior section one objective was to "establish a more competitive trust operation to support bank growth." Several goals can de derived from this objective. They are:

- Increase the book value of trust assets 25% annually.

- Implement specified computer system enhancements to support competitive trust services by June 1985.

- Improve trust profitability by $500,000 in 1985 by controlling operating revenues and expenses.

A word of caution. We find that establishing preliminary goals this early is risky. The risk in quantifying goals too early is that quantified matters have a tendency to become permanent commitments rather than *preliminary* positions. The act of quantifying and dating this objective gives it this added sense of permanence. Therefore, we prefer to halt the process with preliminary objectives and withhold quantifying and dating them until we have formalized the mission and objectives (Chapter 5).

Planning Assumptions

The executive planning committee and the planning officer work together to prepare a set of initial planning assumptions. These address both the external economic forces to which the bank is most sensitive and the critical internal forces. For example, preliminary assumptions should be developed for such areas as:

External Forces	Internal Forces
• Economic growth	• Personnel levels
• Interest rates	• Salary structures
• Inflation rates	• Hardware and software acquisition
• Regulatory changes	• Facility configuration
• Unemployment	• Deposit growth rates
• Technology	• Loan volume growth rates
• Competition	• New products/services
• Demographics	
• Money supply	

The resulting set of planning assumptions will form a common base for the rest of the planning effort. Chemical Bank's recent strategic plan includes the assumption that deregulation..."will come tomorrow." As a result, its plan is to position itself as a competitor in the financial services industry, not merely in the banking industry. Each area within the bank will then be able to develop its strategies based on common views of interest rates, inflation rates, competition, etc. As the strategic planning process develops through environmental scanning and internal analysis, the set of assumptions will likely expand and individual assumptions will need to be revised. After revision, all units are notified of the revision and are requested to update their strategies accordingly. Thus, each unit is always working with the same view of the external environment and the same internal constraints. A segment of a typical set of planning assumptions is portrayed in Figure 2-4.

Defining Strategic Business Units

We define a Strategic Business Unit (SBU) as a segment of the bank whose services, market environment, marketing force, competitors and customers are significantly different from the rest of the bank's activities — so different that it requires its own set of strategies. Typical SBUs at a smaller bank might include retail, commercial, trust, cash management/brokerage, credit card, escrow and administration.

Key to the definition of SBU is the *significantly different* nature of its business compared with the rest of the bank's activities. Each unit is so different that it would be quite unrealistic to develop one set of strategies to simultaneously deal with each of them. For example, recognizing that the retail segment serves a dissimilar market, offers separate services and faces different competitors than the commercial segment of the bank, reinforces the need for separate strategies for each.

Location of the SBU within the bank's formal structure is important. Figure 2-5 shows a segment of a typical bank organization chart. The question to be answered is what level should we designate as the SBU level? The bank level is probably too high and at the municipal bond level is too low for most smaller banks. Too much detail would be required to develop separate sets of strategies for municipal bonds and commercial paper. The trust services level appears to be the most appropriate, particularly for small financial institutions.

CANYON COMMUNITY BANK OF ARIZONA
1984-86 BUSINESS PLAN
PLANNING ASSUMPTIONS

As input to your planning process, we have developed some key assumptions about the general economic activity for you to use in formulating your unit plan. All units should use these assumptions regarding inflation, GNP and the other factors given here for consistency throughout the bank.

Growth — The economy will experience real growth of about 3% in each year of the plan.

Inflation — Overall inflation rates as measured by the Consumer Price Index are expected to be:

1984	5%
1985	6%
1986	6%

Unemployment — Growth in new jobs will exceed the number of labor force entrants and the 1983 unemployment rate of 10.1% will decline to 9.5% in 1984, 9.0% in 1985 and 8.7% in 1986.

Construction — Private housing starts will remain at nearly the 1983 level of 2.1 million. Early indications however based on permit applications show that 1984 starts could easily reach 2.2 million and show a small decline from that level to about 2 million by 1986.

Interest rate — Short-term rates are expected to increase to 100 basis points due to pressure for stabilizing the dollar. Long-term rates will delay this trend by six months and will increase by 85 points to 95 points in the next two years. Rates on average for short-term money will be 9.5% for 1984, 9.8% in 1985, and 10% in 1986.

Capital expenditures — The required return on invested capital for discretionary projects should be at least 15% after taxes.

Personnel levels — The present bank personnel level of 211 will be maintained throughout 1984. Hiring will be based solely on attrition.

Salary levels — Average bank personnel salaries will increase by 7.5% during 1984 and 8% in 1985.

FIGURE 2-4

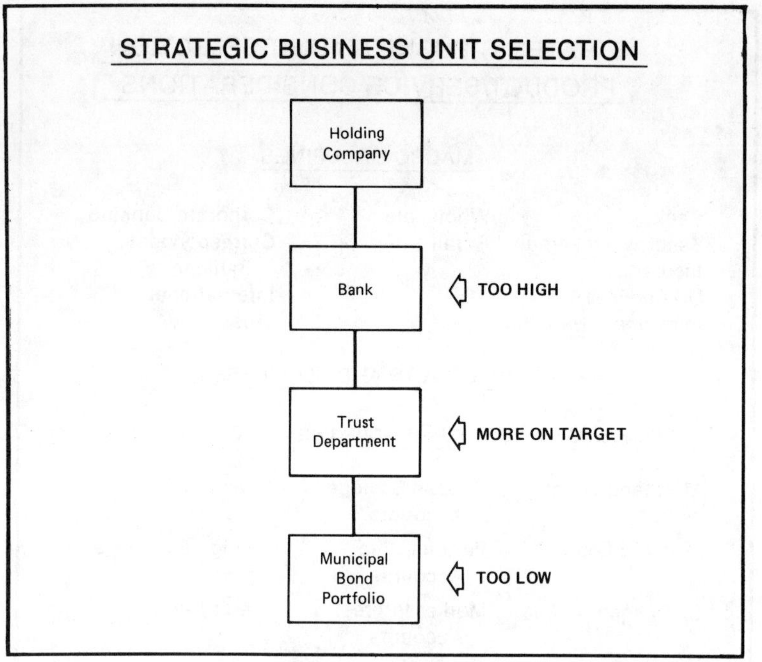

FIGURE 2-5

Our discussion, thus far, of SBU identification and location has focused on segments currently in place within the bank. But you must also consider SBUs anticipated in the future and identify them as early as possible. After examining the strengths, weaknesses, opportunities and threats (SWOTs) in Chapters 3 and 4, you may be prompted to eliminate existing SBUs and identify new ones. As you formulate objectives, goals and strategies, it may be necessary to make adjustments to the bank's SBU configuration. Figure 2-6 identifies some products and services which should be taken into account in establishing the bank's strategic business units. Also, various summary classifications of bank operations can assist management conceptualize business unit identification.

Designating Roles and Responsibilities

Earlier in this chapter, we discussed the roles and responsibilities of the Chief Executive Officer, the board of directors and the executive planning committee. Other key participants in the process are the bank planning officer, SBU managers and outside consultants.

STRATEGIC BUSINESS UNIT SELECTION
PRODUCT/SERVICE CONSIDERATIONS

MACRO GROUPINGS

Bank	Wholesale	Corporate Banking
Security Brokerage	Retail	Correspondent Banking
Insurance		International
DP Services		Trust
Investment Banking		

PRODUCTS AND SERVICES

FUNDS USAGE	FUNDS SOURCING	SERVICES
Mortgage Loans	Deposit/Savings Accounts	Investment Accounts
Demand Loans	Various Club Accounts	Foreign Exchange
Installment Loans	Market Interest Accounts	Credit Card
Leasing	Time CD's	Lock Box
Credit Card	IRA's	Cost Management
Export Financing	Keogh Accounts	Travelers Checks
		Loan Servicing
		Secondary Marketing

FIGURE 2-6

Planning officer — The person "in charge" of planning does not develop the plan; instead, he facilitates the effort. The bank CEO and SBU managers are the only ones who are legitimately entitled to plan strategically since they are solely responsible for the outcome.

A failure to understand this fundamental point has led to the demise of many planning officers and planning efforts. Planning officers rarely have the authority, power and political clout to ensure that strategies are implemented and objectives realized. Thus, their proper role is to:

- Develop the planning process.

- Act as a resource and catalyst for the planners.
- Monitor and report progress.

Too often we have seen planning officers and planning departments actually develop the strategic plan and submit it to the CEO and executive planning committee for review and approval. To the planning department it may seem a natural step from preparing the annual budget and profit plan to preparing the strategic plan. However, over the years we have observed that the probability of developing a successful strategic planning climate decreases as the planning officer's organizational autonomy and direct intervention into strategy development increases. We like to compare the role of the planning officer to that of a ship's navigator.

A navigator asks questions of the captain regarding destination, speed and general course to be followed. He collects data about the current position and plots a course. He reports the progress to the officer in charge. He never makes decisions about either the destination or the purpose of the voyage. And he does not exercise authority over the other officers.

Some of the planning officer's specific strategic planning responsibilities are to:

- Develop an effective planning approach.
- Prepare and maintain a corporate planning manual.
- Assist the CEO and executive team in developing the bank's mission, objectives and goals.
- Prepare the annual planning calendar.
- Serve as project coordinator.
- Conduct special studies.
- Critique intermediate planning products, point out conflicts or inconsistencies and advise the committee on options.
- Consolidate the SBU plans into the overall bank strategic plan and coordinate resolution of the differences.
- Develop user requirements for an environmental surveillance system.

In summary, the job of planning officer is not merely to design, install and maintain a formal planning system. He also helps the managers identify the critical issues and provides the best information he can. He must recognize that his task is not simply to find a rational, technical solution but also to discover an approach that is culturally acceptable, politically feasible and economically attainable. The planning officer must realize that there are many planning styles. He must understand planning in all its dimensions and match the planning approach to the needs and capabilities of the bank.

SBU managers — Role of the SBU managers in the strategic planning process is similar to that of the CEO, except at the lower SBU level. Managers' responsibilities during the development phase are principally to:

- Establish a favorable planning climate within their SBUs.
- Review and approve relevant environmental assumptions and forecasts.
- Establish SBU objectives and goals.
- Develop SBU strategies.
- Monitor SBU progress.

To be successful, the SBU managers need the ability to think strategically and creatively; to look beyond narrow interests; to understand the bank's economic situation; to balance the short-term with the long-term; and to be realistic yet imaginative.

The SBU managers can expect assistance from the planning officer in identifying the critical issues, collecting and analyzing data, developing systems to monitor and follow up. However, the ultimate responsibility for the SBUs' plans and their accomplishment rests with each manager, not the planning officer.

Outside consultants — Although formation of strategies is entirely an internal affair, increasingly there are cases where inputs and insights from other sources are needed. One source of such inputs is the outside consultant.

If you need a consultant, then you should specifically define his role in the planning process. A professional consultant can bring to the strategic planning process a variety of experiences, such as:

- Past situations dealing with similar problems and processes.
- Team approach, which combines consultants and bank personnel.
- Proven, cost-effective methodology for strategic planning.
- External view of the bank.
- Involvement as a catalyst for planned change.

The responsibilities of bank personnel must not be confused with those of the consultant. In Figure 2-7 we show how and where a consultant can assist the bank during strategic planning. You may not wish to use a consultant during every phase of the plan but this table will contrast the role of the consultant with that of bank personnel in each phase.

Although much has been written on how to select a consultant, we think the following are the most significant selection issues:

- Will the consultants assist in actually implementing the plan?
- What are their experiences?
- Can they provide references?
- Does their firm have the management expertise to draw from to deal with your special problems?
- Are they backed by adequate technology?
- Are they going to train the bank personnel so they can carry on when the consultants leave?
- Do they have a track record of adding value on strategic planning projects?

After selecting the consultant, you must keep in mind:

- It's the bank's plan not the consultant's.

USE OF STRATEGIC CONSULTANTS IN BANK STRATEGIC PLANNING

Possible Consultant Assistance	Bank Responsibility
I. Organization Phase	
• Define planning process manual and document with planning	• Review and approve work program
• Develop work program	• Designate: - planning committee members - planning officer - SBUs
• Define characteristics of: - planning committee - planning officer	• Review and revise planning calendar
• Identification of external and internal data	• Assist in developing data requirements list
• Conduct training seminars	
II. Environmental Analysis and Forecast	
• Identification and analysis of economic factors	• Evaluation and forecast of environmental factors
• Analysis of relevant regulations	• Preparation of market outlook
• Analysis of technological trends	• Evaluation of opportunities and threats
• Market studies	• Preparation of final environmental forecast report
• Analysis of markets and segments	
• Analysis of opportunities and threats	
III. Internal Analysis and Position Assessment	
• Analysis of competitors	• Preparation for competition and customer profiles
• Analysis of customers	
• Analysis of industry success factors	• Identification of industry key success factors
• Profit improvement assistance	• Evaluation of company strengths and weaknesses
• Identification of strengths and weaknesses	• Preparation of final environmental forecast report

FIGURE 2-7

Possible Consultant Assistance	Bank Responsibility
IV. Objectives and Goals Development	
• Assist with development of overall business mission • Assist in consolidating objectives from external and internal analyses • Provide methodology for: - Identifying key objectives - assuring completeness and consistency of objectives • Assist in reviewing, analyzing and evaluating objectives and goals	• Develop overall business mission • Consolidate objectives from external and internal analyses • Identify key objectives • Assure completeness and consistency of objectives • Develop quantitive goals for each objective • Communicate objectives and goals
V. Strategy Development	
• Provide methodology for: - Identifying and analyzing strategies - documenting and consolidating strategies - evaluating strategies • Identify areas for strategy formation • Survey division/departments for strategies • Assist with evaluation of strategies through the use of mechanized models • Assist with the review of alternative strategies for completeness, consistency and relevance	• Formulate strategy • Document strategy inputs, risks, resources and likelihood of success • Evaluate proposed strategies • Document finalized strategies
VI. Plan Development	
• Preparation of supporting financial information • Financial projections and modeling	• Content of financial projections • Preparation of financial summaries • Preparation of executive summaries • Preparation of final strategic plan

FIGURE 2-7 (Continued)

- You must be able to carry on after the consultants are finished.

- It's a team effort, combining contributions of bank personnel and consultants.

Developing Work Programs and Timetable

The work program is a tool used to determine the manpower required for the project and to provide a means to monitor progress. The planning officer prepares the program to communicate the details of the planning process and its interdependencies. A good work program breaks a large, complex effort into understandable, manageable tasks, thus lessening the frustration, fear and resentment commonly observed at the beginning of any major effort.

Typically, the work program includes:

- Specific tasks and steps needed to accomplish each phase of strategic planning.

- Responsibility for completion of each task.

- Estimated effort required to complete the tasks.

- Estimated start and completion dates.

Figure 2-8 is an example of a segment from a work program for a community bank.

Identifying Preliminary Data Requirements

The next two phases of the strategic planning process — environmental scanning (Chapter 3) and the internal analysis/position assessment (Chapter 4) — require significant quantities of data which usually are not readily available. Therefore, a data collection effort must be initiated. Early identification of at least the major data requirements will allow more time for fact-gathering and will eliminate later delays in the planning process if key data are missing. Individuals should be assigned specific responsibility for the collection, analysis, summarization and reporting. Figure 2-9 shows a *portion* of a typical bank data requirements list. The Appendix at the end of this monograph lists some of the sources of external data for U.S. commercial banks.

CATTLEMAN'S BANK OF HOUSTON
STRATEGIC PLANNING WORK PROGRAM AND TIMETABLE

DESCRIPTION	ASSIGNED TO	ESTIMATED WORK DAYS TOTAL	BANK	OUTSIDE CONSULTANTS	START DATE	COMPLETION DATE	APR 30	MAY 7	14	21	28
II. ENVIRONMENTAL ANALYSIS FORECAST											
A. Examine Economic, Regulatory & Political Influence											
1. Document government regulations which affect or may potentially affect the bank.	J. Dow	4	3	1	May 7	May 14					
2. Document social developments and demographics which may impact the bank.	J. Dow	3	3		May 7	May 14					
3. Document developments in the economy which will have a direct or indirect effect on the bank.				1	May 7	May 21					
B. Examine Technology											
1. Review and summarize technological changes which affect operations.	M. Avolio	10	5	5	April 30	May 14					
2. List major areas to be addressed.	M. Avolio	2	1	1	April 30	May 14					
C. Examine Market Outlook											
1. Prepare formal analysis of the market:	J. Edwards	23	15	8	May 14	May 28					
• Describe the industry by external forces (e.g., trade associations, SIC categories, competitive structure).					May 14	May 28					
• Identify market segments (in term of product line, production facilities, distribution and sales methods).					May 14	May 28					
• Determine market penetration.					May 14	May 28					
• Determine growth rates for the industry and served markets over the past five years (elements such as growth, profits, return on capital).					May 21	May 28					
• Assess important industry and market trends over the last two or three years (qualitative statements).					May 21	May 28					

FIGURE 2-8

PRELIMINARY DATA REQUIREMENTS

Major Competitive Banks

- Total assets: history, market shares, trends
- Total demand deposits: history, market share, trend and time deposits
- Analysis of loan portfolio
- Selected financial statement information and key ratios
- Analysis of services and fees
- Number and location of branches

Regional Demographics

- Population
- Housing
- Overall income/sales
- Labor trends
- Major employers

Internal Bank Data

- Total demand and time deposits by market area and branch
- Loan portfolio analysis
- Key ratios
- Major volumes

Economic Data — Forecasts for planning period:

- Employment
- Interest rates
- Rate of inflation
- Rate of growth in the money supply
- Local economy

Regulatory Data

- Anticipated government actions
- Regulations regarding:
    - Competition from organizations
    - Consumer protection
    - Geographic boundaries
    - New financial services

FIGURE 2-9

Finalize and Communicate

The planning letter is the first major announcement to bank personnel of the upcoming planning effort. We view this letter as the critical first step in establishing the right planning attitudes among employees and in creating the desired planning climate within the bank. The major objectives of this letter should be to:

- Communicate the CEO's support and commitment.
- Emphasize the importance of strategic planning.
- Encourage involvement and support.
- Emphasize the expected benefits.

This letter should come from the CEO and be addressed to the management team. Figure 2-10 illustrates a typical bank planning letter.

The culmination of initiating a strategic plan is to finalize the results, consolidate them into a planning manual and distribute the manual to the appropriate individuals.

Finalizing the planning process essentially involves two major steps:

- Verify that the whole process has been documented and is in writing
- Have the whole process reviewed and approved by the Executive Planning Committee

Without documentation, the bank's efforts would not be effective. Staff would be operating under various assumptions about what is expected of them and what to expect from others. As a result, many tasks will be duplicated while other citical tasks would be ignored.

The review and approval process puts top management's "stamp of approval" on the approach, thereby relieving the planning officer of responsibility for it. Senior management's approval is critical to avoid the appearance that this is the planning officer's "show." The CEO and the executive planning committee must accept and demonstrate full responsibility for the designated methodology.

PLANNING LETTER

HOPI NATIONAL BANK OF SCOTTSDALE
JUNE 11, 1983

FROM: CHIEF EXECUTIVE OFFICER

TO: SENIOR VICE PRESIDENTS

- EXECUTIVE VICE PRESIDENTS AND CASHIER
- TRUST VICE PRESIDENT
- SENIOR LOAN OFFICER
- BROKERAGE VICE PRESIDENT

SUBJECT: STRATEGIC PLANNING

Hopi National Bank has been successful over the years because its managers have exhibited capability in running the business.

As competition becomes stronger and the economic, technological and regulatory environment becomes more complex, effective planning is increasingly important to assure continued growth. These factors, and the essential involvement of more managers in the planning process, increase the need for a systematic and comprehensive approach to planning.

The strategic planning process requires your active involvement. The strategic planning horizon will be five years. A conference will be scheduled in the near future to further discuss this most important undertaking.

Attached is a statement of preliminary objectives developed by the Planning Committee. These objectives are broad in scope and will serve as a starting point in developing more specific objectives, goals and strategies in each of your strategic business units. Also attached are planning assumptions to assist you in developing your unit objectives and goals.

Good planning at Hopi National will be an important cornerstone for a good future.

Chief Executive Officer

Attachments

FIGURE 2-10

The planning manual provides guidance to everyone involved in preparing the strategic plan. Initially it contains just the output from the organizing and initiating efforts. Figure 2-11 illustrates the initial sections of the manual. As the strategic plan is developed the planning manual should be a complete summary of the process and an integrated collection of the outputs. The manual is then distributed to the appropriate personnel. The completed planning manual is discussed and illustrated in Chapter 7.

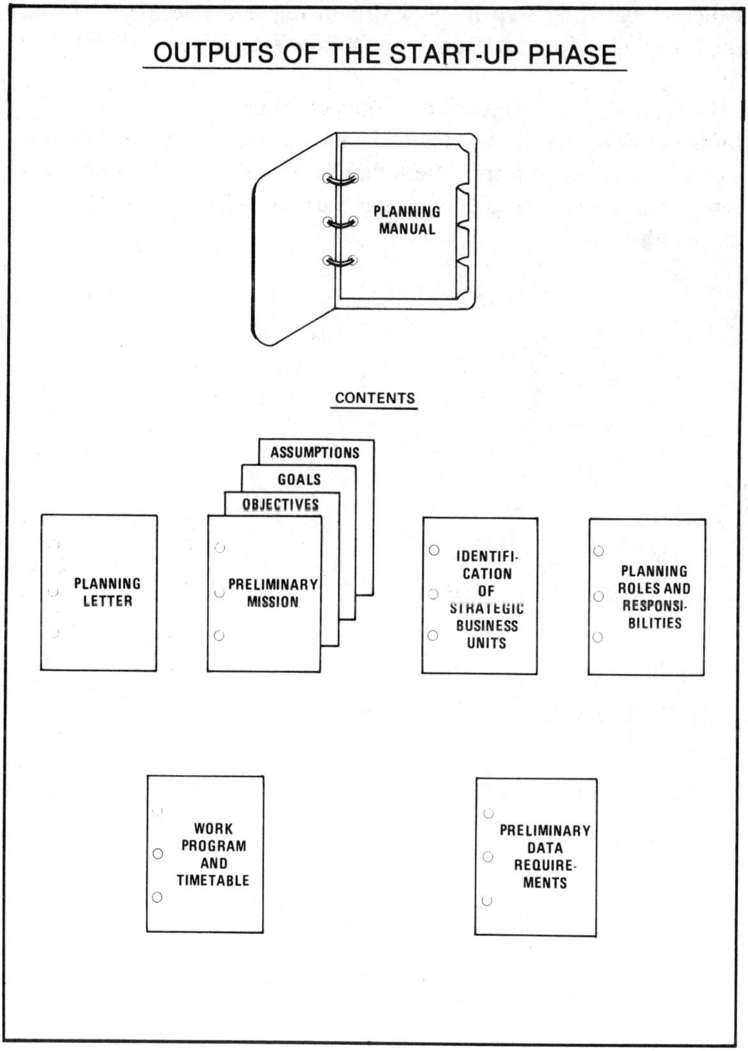

FIGURE 2-11

Summary

Overall, this chapter, longest in the monograph, has been about developing commitment to the strategic planning process among all the key people who are the CEO's support team. The planning to plan effort is the crux of developing this commitment. We have provided detailed instructions on identifying roles and responsibilities, setting the mission, goals and objectives, and addressing the issues of assumptions and outside consultants. Communication is the critical final step in your organizing and initiating efforts, which explains the importance of the planning letter and manual.

If organizing and initiating strategic planning is cut short, the whole planning effort is likely to be ineffective. Effective strategic planning requires an atmosphere that facilitates meaningful discussion of bank issues, and encourages participation in the challenges that lie ahead.

3 ENVIRONMENTAL SCANNING

"Forecasting is difficult, especially about the future."
... Anonymous

Successful strategic planning requires scanning the bank's external environment and analyzing its internal situation. External scanning looks at the environment and attempts to identify those threats and opportunities outside the bank. Internal analysis, on the other hand, looks at the bank's current situation and identifies its internal strengths and weaknesses.

These inward and outward views are the backbone of the strategic plan. They are critical in developing realistic strategies which explicitly match the bank's strengths and weaknesses to the environmental threats and opportunities.

This chapter examines the external forces that impact the bank and discusses our approach to environmental scanning. Chapter 4 examines the critical forces inside the bank and discusses internal analysis and position assessment.

External Environment

The external environment is a complex host of largely uncontrollable factors which can influence the bank's strategic decisions and, ultimately, its success or failure. Historically, banks faced a stable environment. The industry was highly regulated, competition from non-banks was limited, interest rates and inflation rates were stable, and bankers could confine their environmental awareness to their geographic vicinity. The potential external forces influencing the bank were both easy to identify and relatively predictable.

As a result, bankers spent little time identifying and evaluating their potential impact. In fact, an attitude of generally ignoring the external environment was not all that unreasonable, given its stability. Today, however, bankers no longer enjoy the luxury of a stable external environment. Any banker who ignores the effect of forces outside his control is almost certain to miss the opportunities of the 80s.

In this chapter, we attempt to impose a structure on the external environment. We see today's banker facing two categories of external forces. First, the *remote environment,* which comprises those forces over which the smaller bank does not possess the strength to exert any meaningful reciprocal influence. Second, the *proximity environment,* which comprises forces over which the bank may exert some influence. Figure 3-1 portrays our view of the external environment and some of the major forces impacting the bank.

A BANK'S VIEW OF THE EXTERNAL WORLD

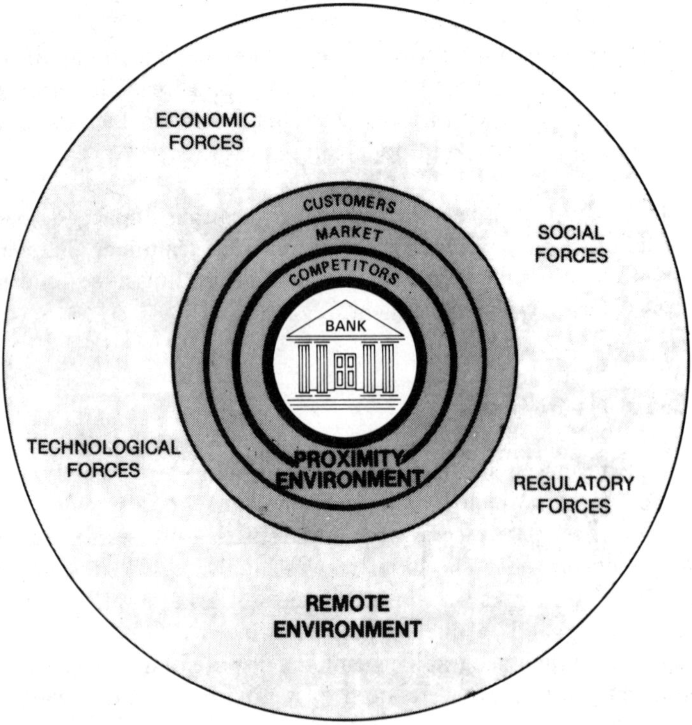

EXTERNAL ENVIRONMENT

FIGURE 3-1

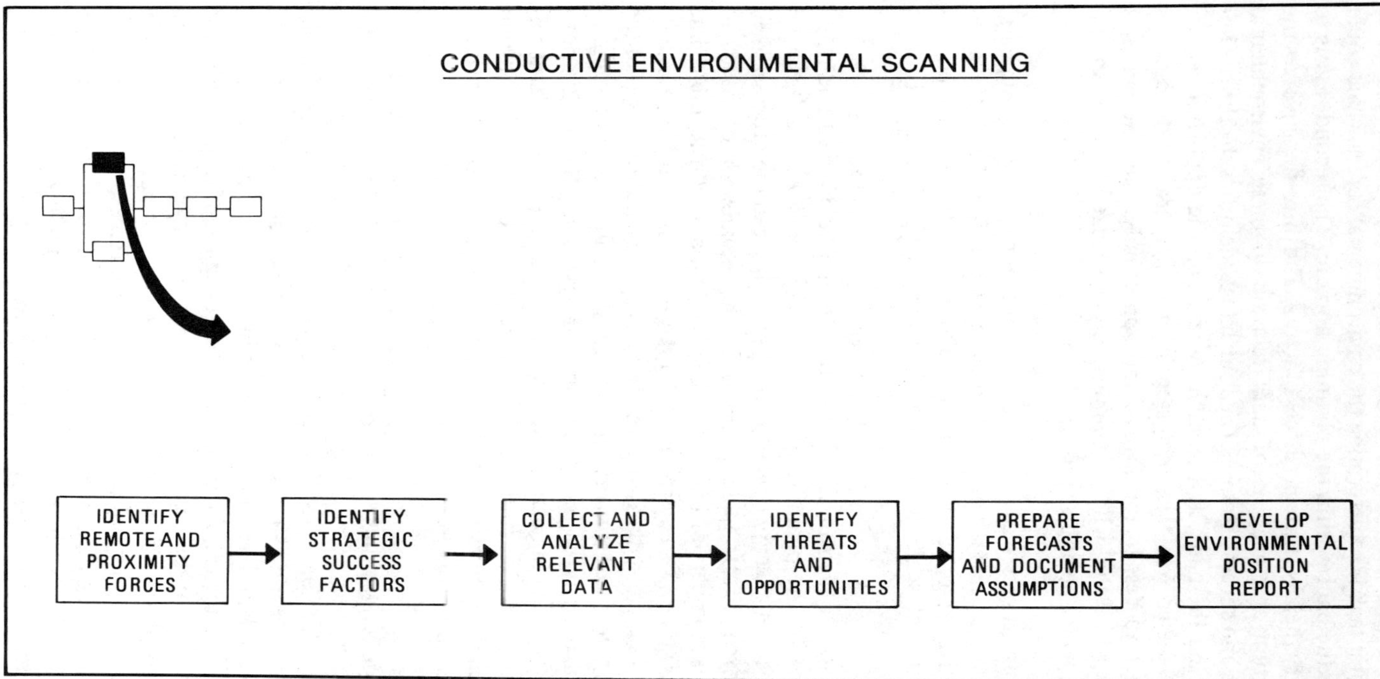
CONDUCTIVE ENVIRONMENTAL SCANNING
IDENTIFY REMOTE AND PROXIMITY FORCES
IDENTIFY STRATEGIC SUCCESS FACTORS
COLLECT AND ANALYZE RELEVANT DATA
IDENTIFY THREATS AND OPPORTUNITIES
PREPARE FORECASTS AND DOCUMENT ASSUMPTIONS
DEVELOP ENVIRONMENTAL POSITION REPORT

FIGURE 3-2

The environmental scanning process is illustrated in Figure 3-2. The first task is to determine the environmental forces which could affect the bank within the planning horizon. The second task is to identify the key strategic success factors. The third step involves the collection and analysis of data relevant to these environmental forces and success factors. The fourth task identifies the threats imposed on the bank by the environment and the opportunities for profitable growth. The fifth step includes preparation of forecasts for each success factor, threat, and opportunity. The sixth and last task brings the whole scanning process together into an environmental position report.

As noted previously, the linear presentation of the environmental scanning process is not intended to represent something that is not repetitive or dynamic in nature. On the contrary, effective environmental scanning requires constant rethinking and conceptualizing.

Although environmental scanning should be directed and coordinated by the planning officer, it is absolutely essential that all members of executive management participate in the process. Well organized efforts include not only the assignment of issues to various members of bank management, but also considerable time for discussion of environmental analysis by the planning committee. This is particularly true in the earlier identification stages of the process as well as in the latter stages as results are being summarized and analyzed for the purpose of developing the bank's position. The planning officer, however, should serve as the central collection point for strategically important environmental information, making certain that all significant findings are appropriately disseminated.

Remote Environmental Issues

The "remote environment" refers to those forces which originate beyond the bank's control. These forces would include, for example, interest rates, changes in federal and state regulations, and technological changes. These forces can significantly alter the very nature of the banking business; and yet any one bank is essentially helpless to influence them. As a result, considerable attention is warranted to monitor and analyze these forces so when changes actually occur bank management is not caught unprepared. They have anticipated the nature of the change and have positioned the bank to deal with the new environment.

But, because the remote environment is complex, management often finds it difficult to forecast changes and to anticipate their impact on the bank. Often the remote environment is viewed as inherently unpredictable, and therefore little time is spent trying to understand and anticipate major trends. As a result, when such major changes occur, they are unprepared. Their bank is not positioned to respond immediately. Instead of convincing them of the need for environmental scanning, unanticipated changes usually reinforce the belief in the unpredictability of the future.

Thus, bankers say their efforts are more profitably spent on internal issues such as cost reduction, marketing and personnel than on anticipating changes in remote forces. Our consulting experiences have convinced us that his view is not justified if the proper approach is used to analyze the remote environment. Only very large cost reductions or very successful marketing efforts could overcome the profits generated from a correctly anticipated change of a single, significant external force, such as interstate branch banking legislation or a turning point in the economy.

From our consulting experiences, we have identified four categories of remote environmental forces most critical to the long-term survival and profitability of a smaller bank. They are:

- Economic forces
- Regulatory forces
- Social forces
- Technological forces

For each of these categories, we have prepared a checklist of the more common issue areas or trends. Figures 3-3 through 3-7 illustrate these considerations. The lists are not complete, but are intended to provide examples of the kinds of issues that would be included in each category. The goal for your bank is to identify those economic forces most critical for your long-term economic survival. For example, if your bank is located in a rural agricultural area, then trends in farm commodity prices are probably more critical to your success than trends in urban housing starts. Chapter 6 will provide some additional insight into the techniques for identifying and determining the degree to which bank profits are sensitive to external forces.

Economic Forces

Economic forces refer to the nature and direction of the economy in which the bank operates. Since financial performance and customer behavior are largely influenced by economic forces, it is essential that every banker understand the economic trends that impact his bank.

Most bankers today question to what extent they stake the future of their bank on their knowledge of economic forces. There are many recent and notable examples where bankers have overrelied on their economic knowledge and had disasterous results. Consider interest rates. There have been any number of financial institutions who bet on declining interest rates in a time of runaway inflation. They frequently lent long with fixed rate loans and were squeezed unmercifully.

Figure 3-3 identifies a number of the economic forces which should be considered in conducting any environmental analysis.

REPRESENTATIVE ECONOMIC FORCES

- Interest rates
- Inflation rates
- Corporate and personal tax regulation changes
- Socioeconomic
- Specific industry outlooks
- Employment
- Acquisition threats and opportunities
- Government spending
- Federal deficits
- Retail sales
- Housing starts
- Investment trends and investor confidence
- Wholesale sales
- Economic growth

FIGURE 3-3

This list is by no means complete. Specific economic forces can occur in one segment of American industry that can have significant impact on the banking community. For example, consider Penn Square National Bank. When oil prices dropped dramatically as a result of a world petroleum glut, many oil and gas companies lost money and even went bankrupt. Penn Square's inability to repay their creditors resulted in their collapse because they risked considerable portions of its capital on their knowledge of oil and gas. Others that have experienced significant impact are: Continental Illinois National Bank & Trust Co., Abilene National Bank, Chase Manhatten and Seafirst National Bank.

Regulatory Forces

Banks are clearly very dependent on federal and state banking regulations. Thus, strategic planning must incorporate anticipated regulatory changes. The banker's job is to identify which laws and regulations are most likely to change within the planning horizon and how specifically those changes will impact profitability.

By way of illustration, consider the Monetary Control Act of 1980. This act subjected all depository institutions, including savings and loans and credit unions, to Federal Reserve requirements and mandated the Fed to start charging customers for services, such as check clearing. Many commercial banks which understood the implications of the Fed becoming a competitor moved quickly to position themselves in the check processing business. The result was that the Feds lost market share to these banks in 1982, and the banks enjoyed the cost savings and correspondent relationships associated with the bilateral clearing of checks with each other.

Figure 3-4 identifies major areas of bank regulation and areas where regulatory changes should be considered in the strategic planning process. Figure 3-5 highlights a few of the major regulations and regulatory agencies currently impacting the banking industry.

REPRESENTATIVE REGULATORY FORCES

- Holding company legislation
- Capital adequacy requirements
- Liquidity requirements
- Branching regulation
- Services/product legislation
- Regulatory reporting requirements
- Tax legislation
- Interest rate regulations
- Acquisition regulations
- Antitrust
- Lending legislation
- EFT and ATM legislation
- Bank examination requests
- Minimum wage
- Affirmative action

FIGURE 3-4

U.S. REGULATORY ENVIRONMENT

Regulations

AREA IMPACTED	MAJOR RESTRICTIONS	DESCRIPTION
Geographic	• McFadden Act	Limits geographic expansion
	• Bank Holding Company Act (including Douglas Amendments)	Limits geographic expansion via ownership
Rates	• Regulation Q	Deposit rate ceilings (until 1986)
	• State Usury Laws	Set interest rate ceilings on consumer lending
Activities	• Regulation D	Reserve requirement
	• Regulation R	Disallows interlocking relationships between security dealers and member banks
	• Glass Steagall	Disallows security underwriting by deposit taking banks
	• Bank Holding Company Act (including Douglas Amendment)	Limits allowable services and business functions
	• Community Reinvestment Act	Use of deposit funds
	• Other major restrictions	Limits on loan amounts based on Capital and bank size Prohibition against equity participation
Consumers	• Regulation Z	Truth in lending

Regulators*

REGULATORS	NATIONAL BANKS	STATE MEMBER BANKS	INSURED NONMEMBER BANKS	NONINSURED BANKS
Comptroller of the Currency	C,E,F,J			
Federal Reserve	E,F,R,J	E,F,R,J	F,R,J	J
Federal Deposit Insurance Corporation	E,F,J	F,F,J	E,F,J	
State Banking Division		C,E,F,R,J	C,E,F,R,J	C,E,F,R,J

*Key to Symbols

(C) Chartered by
(E) Examined by
(F) Files reports with
(R) Reserves required by
(J) Within the Jurisdiction of

FIGURE 3-5

Social Forces

Social forces encompass the beliefs, values, attitudes, opinions and lifestyles which exist in a bank's external environment.

Major areas of social trends are shown in Figure 3-6. Much has been written about the areas and we will not elaborate further here. The challenge for bankers today is to sift out the relevant forces, identify any trends and relate them to the bank.

REPRESENTATIVE SOCIAL FORCES

- Consumer attitudes
- Lifestyle trends
- Quality of life issues
- Demographic changes
- Changing work and social ethics
- Religious movements
- Ethnic issues and trends

FIGURE 3-6

An excellent illustration of banks observing consumer attitudes and adjusting their strategy accordingly can be seen in the recent moves to lure and serve the more affluent customers. Recognizing that their wealthy customers didn't appreciate waiting in long teller lines and being treated as though they were bad check writers, many banks have recently rolled out the carpet. First Interstate Bank of Oregon launched its Private Banking Division in 1982. The program offered a private teller for high net worth customers, an attractive line of credit that could be activated at any time with only a phone call, credit cards with expanded limits and seminars on finanical topics of general interest. First Interstate believes such sensitivity to the market will pay off since most of its retail profit comes from a small percentage of its customers. First is not alone in red carpet banking. Others include Citibank, Morgan Guaranty, Chase Manhattan, Bank of California and many others.

Technological Forces

Bankers must be aware of changes in technology since such changes spawn new markets, new services and new delivery systems. With the rapid pace of technological change, a bank could find itself obsolete without any provision for considering technology in its strategic planning process. Given the lead times and capital requirements necessary to incorporate new technology, successful banks will be those who anticipate and monitor technological advances and actively incorporate them into their thinking.

The impact of technology is particularly significant in the area of automated delivery systems. Consider the highly publicized comparison of Citicorp vs. Bank of America. Citicorp started installing automated teller machines in 1977 and recently had approximately 500 throughout the city of New York. Bank of America, in comparison, has been slow to adopt technology and has recently had to deal with the high spiralling costs of having an extensive branch-oriented delivery system. The result at Bank of America has been a rapid and extensive investment in new technology and a consolidation of its branch locations, a blitz necessitated by an ever changing computer technology and competitive pressures from within and outside the state of California.

Figure 3-7 identifies a few of the technological areas where banks are currently dealing with new forces in electronic banking.

REPRESENTATIVE TECHNOLOGICAL FORCES

- Hardware trends
- Software trends
- Home banking
- ATM's
- Customer information files
- On-line terminals
- Electronic funds transfer

FIGURE 3-7

Proximity Environment Issues

The proximity environment consists of those forces which are within the bank's immediate situation, the most prominent of which are:

- Competition
- Market
- Customers

These are distinguished from the remote forces because the bank can exert considerably more influence over them. For example, your competition may decide to install ATMs simply because your bank installed them. Or, you institute a check cashing fee for non-customers as a part of an overall campaign to encourage them to move their accounts to your bank. In both instances, not only were the bank's actions influenced by factors in the environment, but also the bank directly affected the environment.

The proximity environment provides many of the most exciting challenges facing bankers, especially if the bank is going to translate actions and reactions by these forces into profitable strategies. This requires the banker to know his competition, his market and his customers.

Competitor Profiling

The purposes of profiling the bank's competitors are:

- Identify competitors.
- Determine competitor strengths and weaknesses.
- Heighten the bank's awareness of competitor actions.

Historically, competitor identification was easy. Bankers knew who they were up against. Today, however, identifying competition is not as easy. With the transformation of conventional banking into a competitive array of financial services, your immediate competitors could easily include representatives from such diverse institutions as:

- Credit unions
- Savings and loan associations
- Money market funds
- Brokerage houses
- Insurance companies
- Travel card companies
- Retail merchants

The starting point is the bank's mission. It defines the bank's niche within the environment. It identifies *who* the bank is, *what* markets it's going to serve and *how* it's going to serve them. This should provide some basis for identifying the bank's competitors. Is Merrill Lynch, Pierce, Fenner & Smith Inc. a genuine competitor for your bank? The answer depends on what niche you see your bank servicing.

Once competitors are identified, portfolios are prepared and maintained for each. This step requires extensive data gathering on both quantitative and qualitative factors. Figure 3-8 illustrates the kinds of data that would normally be gathered. The sources of this data include external sources listed in the Appendix and potentially all bank personnel including tellers, loan officers and managers.

DATA FOR COMPETITIVE PROFILE

- Financial condition
- Size
- Location of main office and branches
- Range of services
- Quality of services
- Market segments served
- Market share
- Use of high technology
- Image
- ATMs
- Credit standards
- Quality of personnel
- Price of services
- Advertising effectiveness
- Cross-sell effectiveness
- Market advantages/disadvantages
- Market segmentation effectiveness
- Names and backgrounds of directors and top management
- Market strengths (dominates or has a unique appeal to)
- Innovativeness (services, delivery, promotion, marketing)
- Promotional efforts
- New market alliances
- Major accounts

FIGURE 3-8

Based on the data gathered, a competitive profile is prepared for each competitor. The profile summarizes the research and identifies your perceptions of their strengths and weaknesses. Figure 3-9 portrays a *portion* of such a report on a competitor community bank.

ILLUSTRATIVE COMPETITIVE PROFILE
NAPA VALLEY NATIONAL BANK

Background

- Formed in 1985
- $85 million in assets
- 6 branches
- 102 employees

Significant Strengths

- Strong community identity and image.
- Modern, attractive physical facilities.
- Napa's six locations give it a broad base for providing service
- Strong, active board of directors
- Apparent commitment to providing quality service
- Knowledgeable chief executive and president

Significant Weaknesses

- Lack of depth in middle management.
- Recent loan losses have significantly weakened capital position
- Some recent loss of image in community due to computer problems
- Strong imbalance of rate sensitive assets to rate sensitive liabilities

Financial Condition

- Current shareholders provide a capacity for obtaining new equity capital should this be necessary.
- Marginal fee income.
- Earnings situation facilitated by a better than average base of low-cost deposits.
- Currently very sensitive to increases in prime rate.

FIGURE 3-9

Products and Relative Market Share

	Amount ($ 000)	Estimated Market Share (%)	Comments
Loans			
• Real Estate	$ 38,000	25%	• Heavy position in the subdivision
• Line of Credit	$ 12,000	15%	
• Installment Loans	$ 10,000	15%	
• Corporate	$ 15,000		• Aggressively pursuing
Demand Deposits	$ 25,000	8%	
Savings	$ 24,000		
Money Market	$ 12,000	10%	
Cert. of Deposit	$ 10,000		
Credit Card		10-15%	• Uses services of correspondent

Organization and Managerial Ability

- Organization seems to have fairly good unity of purpose.
- Jeffrey Stennett (President and CEO) has strong leadership qualities and is respected for his managerial skills.
- Three of six senior officers have extensive banking experience.
- Recently formed holding company, although currently only a legal entity without a separate management team.
- Verne Naito (Loans) and Mark Avolio (Trust), are aggressive and tough bankers who could become even tougher competition.
- Personable teller force that actively cross-sells.

Staying Power

- Despite recent loan losses, Napa has an adequate capital base.
- Management and Board are committed to surviving in the banking industry and maintain the organization's identity.

Ability to Grow/Adapt to Change

- Napa has limited ability (or interest) to expand geographically beyond immediate market territory.
- Adaptive process within the bank is slow but consistent.

Quick Response Capability

- Napa would likely counter any pricing moves to gain market share quickly by repricing its own products and services.
- Slow to develop and market any new products.

FIGURE 3-9 (Continued)

Competitor profiling does not end with issuing profile reports. For profiling to become effective, it must be carried on continuously. The job description of every key person in the bank should include monitoring the competition and keeping executive management informed about the competitive environment. Gradually, you will build up a comprehensive profile on each competitor that is comparable to your market and customer profiles.

Regardless of the form adopted for profiling, an organized and systematic approach to competitive analysis is absolutely essential. Competition is too critical a force to be addressed haphazardly.

Market Profiling

Objectives of market profiling are to identify, analyze, and forecast key marketplace factors which may affect the bank within the planning horizon. In addition, we want to develop an understanding of the marketplace in order to recognize threats and opportunities as they occur.

We use the term "market" in a broad way. It includes:

- Total market: That which is available to all financial institutions.
- Market segment: Any part of the total market which can be separately identified.
- Markets served: A market segment in which the bank actually competes.

Profiling the market includes examining each of these.

The *total market* is evaluated to answer such questions as:

- What is the size of the total market?
- Is it growing or declining?
- Are major changes occurring?
- Are major changes expected? What and when?
- What are the important characteristics of the market?

- What are the driving forces within the market?
- What environmental forces threaten the total market?
- Can the total market be realistically segmented?

The sources for most total market information would be external and similar to those used in the economic forecast. External sources include published material from Federal Home Loan Bank Board, Federal Reserve Banks, U.S. Department of Commerce and FDIC. See Appendix for other sources of information.

The results from the total market study are summarized and included as a section within the market position report. Typically this section would include:

- Data summary.
- Sources identified.
- Identification of critical marketwide driving forces.
- Major conclusions on total market outlook.
- Short and long-term implications for the bank.

An important perspective of the market is derived from *segmenting* it into meaningful groups. This allows for easier assessment of the market status as well as prediction of the impact of changes in other environmental forces. In addition, the strategic plan and its related marketing strategies are developed for market segments rather than the total market.

Market segmenting is not necessarily just a matter of dividing the total market into such categories as: geographic location, account balances, or income levels. Instead, you might assume everyone in the market is unique and thus a market segment in themselves and then look for common characteristics that enable you to aggregate them into meaningful groups. In this way, the market itself tells you how to segment rather than having you arbitrarily segment it according to some timeworn criteria. Important strategic information may be lost if you impose an arbitrary structure for segmenting.

Once the market has been segmented, the task is to research and analyze the population of each to identify its needs. Understanding customer needs is absolutely essential to marketing bank services. People do not purchase bank services per se; instead, they seek ways to satisfy a need.

In addition to identifying consumer needs, the market research and analysis efforts should also gather data to enable the banker to evaluate the future potential of each market segment. The analysis would answer questions similar to those asked about the total market including growth, changes, driving forces and threats. As with the results of total market analysis, the segment analysis is summarized within the market position report.

The reason for profiling the market *segments served* is to determine in which segments the bank is actively involved and the extent of that involvement. This view combined with the segment outlook would reveal changes such as an increasing market share of a declining market segment. Major efforts in this task are to identify the segments served and to determine the bank's market share or penetration. The market share information is generally available from various external sources, e.g., state banking associations.

Conclusions from market examination are also included in the market position report. In particular the report should contain an analysis of the long and short-term impact the total market outlook and the market segment outlook probably will have on the bank in the short-term and the long-term. Special recognition should be made of identified threats and opportunities as they affect markets currently being served. Finally, opportunities identified that have not been addressed should be highlighted so that they are considered when strategies are developed (Chapter 6).

Customer Profile

Achieving an understanding of the nature and characteristics of the bank's customers is perhaps the most valuable benefit from scanning the proximity environment. The bankers must know their customers if they are going to develop realistic strategies to serve their needs. We are continually amazed at how little most bankers know about their customers as a group. Admittedly, most bankers understand each customer individually, but cannot make generalizations about them for the purpose of formulating a strategic plan.

Preparing a customer profile of present and potential customers is a way of organizing a customer analysis to determine common characteristics among them. For example, a customer analysis may reveal that a disproportionate number are employed within one industry or possibly fall into one age bracket, i.e., 50-60 years old. Such information could have significant implications because the bank may be vulnerable to recession in that industry or its customers' retirement from the work force. The pervasiveness of these common characteristics may not have been evident on an individual customer to banker relationship.

The customer profile begins by segmenting existing customers into market groups. At the very least, the segments should identify customers according to:

- Retail (by type of account)
- Commercial (by type of services)
- Trust
- Credit card

Each market group can be further partitioned by account location (eg., main branch, etc.) or by other geographic or demographic criteria useful to the bank.

We have identified five principle types of information about community bank customers that are valuable to strategic planners. The customer profile is organized around these categories:

- Demographic
- Geographic
- Sociological
- Behavioral
- Needs

Figure 3-10 lists some of the information requirements for each category.

CUSTOMER PROFILE CONSIDERATIONS

Demographic

- Occupation
- Income levels
- Nationality
- Education
- Family size
- Social class
- Sex
- Age
- Marital status

Geographic

- Market locations and density
- Urban/rural
- Seasonal patterns
- Transportation patterns

Sociological

- Personality characteristics
- Lifestyle
- Consumption style
- Values

Customer Behavior

- Loyalty
- Services demanded/ignored
- Sensitivity to price changes
- Sensitivity to convenience, quality, etc.
- Sensitivity to personal vs. electronic service

Customer Needs

- Loans
- Various checking, savings accounts
- Trust services
- Cash management
- Escrow services
- IRA's and Keogh plans
- Bank card services

FIGURE 3-10

Developing a useful customer profile suggests either the existence of a well designed central customer information file (CIF) or a fondness for archeology. In our experience, most banks have neither a CIF nor a fondness for digging through a lot of records.

But the inescapable fact is that the bank must "know thy customers."

Many banks have resorted to surveying their customers to identify major characteristics, lifestyles, interests, buying habits, attitudes, etc. However, we must state a word of caution is in order regarding customer surveys. We have seen many banks contract for customer surveys without any idea whatsoever of what information about their customers is really needed to assist them in their strategic planning. In all instances, these banks have been disappointed with the results. Bankers taking the survey approach should first determine what needed data will really make the difference in their development of strategy. For example, a survey might focus on what basis consumers are making their banking decisions. Also, the survey might look at how consumers distinguish the various lenders and the importance they attach to such factors as:

- Marketing/visibility of lender
- Perceived institutional soundness/stability
- Availability of unsecured credit
- Maturity
- Interest rate
- Prior relationship
- Service charges
- Speed of approval
- Ease of access (branch, ATM, home terminal, etc.)

Customer survey data in conjunction with available internal information could make up a customer profile. Customer profiles are used to determine how the bank is perceived in the community and provide clues to the kinds of services wanted. In addition, studying them should answer such questions as:

- What characteristics of the bank's services are most important to the customers?

- Are there any identifiable trends in what customers perceive as important services?

- Are there any unfilled needs?

- What changes in the external environment are affecting our customer's activities with us?

- Is the bank vulnerable to particular environmental changes which impact customers and may not have been identified in other scanning activities?

The conclusions drawn from the customer profiles should be summarized in a customer position report. This report includes summary statistics about market groups and customer profile considerations. In addition, any key customer issues identified during the analysis should be highlighted and included in the eventual environmental position report. Lastly, the report should include a summary of any perceived customer base strengths and weaknesses.

Identification of Strategic Success Factors

Strategic success factors are those few key variables which relate critically and directly to the bank's strategic plan. They are the life and death factors which will determine its future success. Their requirements include:

- Direct relationship to the success of a defined course of action

- Usefulness in motivation

- Controllable

- Macro perspective

- Limited in number

Strategic success factors should invoke an issues orientation that identifies those issues critical to the bank's long-term success or failure. These factors can and should vary depending on how the bank is postured in relation to its remote and proximity environment.

Strategic success factors could include, for example, the following:

- Reduction of interest rate exposure associated with its gap position.
- Ability to convey a full-service image to its customers.
- Ability to raise capital.
- Increased market share in designated areas of the business.
- Ability to diversify into a broader range of financial services.

The identification of these factors as a part of conducting an environmental analysis is absolutely critical. This effort will result in a more meaningful analysis of the environmental forces as they impact the bank by providing a framework of materiality as one undertakes the data collection effort.

Data Collection and Analysis

Beyond the identification of the environmental forces and the strategic success factors, an effective analysis will involve:

- Gathering data
- Analyzing the forces
- Summarizing the results

The preliminary data requirements were identified in Chapter 2 and various sources expanded upon in the Appendix. Although these efforts were previously initiated. External scanning will surface the need for more information. You should anticipate this and coordinate the effort through the planning officer.

Threats and Opportunities

At this point, the environment has been thoroughly scanned. The economic, regulatory, social and technological forces have been analyzed. The bank's competition, markets and customers have been examined and profiled and the significant strategic issues identified. The next task is to bring components of the environment together and summarize the environmental threats and opportunities.

For each threat, the following should be discussed:

- Source of the threat.
- Nature of the threat.
- Impact if the threat materializes.
- Approach for forecasting critical events related to the threat.

For each opportunity, a summary similar to the threats summary should be prepared. The report would include a description and discussion of the nature of the opportunity and a discussion of the general benefits to the bank if the opportunity was pursued. To the extent there are uncertainties related to an opportunity materializing, the methods for determining the likelihood of it actually happening should be discussed.

Forecasts and Assumptions

To assist in assessing the likelihood and magnitude of the bank's threats and opportunities, various forecasts should be prepared. In this process all necessary assumptions should be identified and documented.

Documenting assumptions allows bank management to address their importance and degree of certainty. Counterassumptions can be developed to test their relevance and implied conclusions. The formulation of undocumented assumptions is a risky proposition that can cause disasterous consequences for the bank's strategic planning efforts.

For example, assumptions which might be critical to the bank's forecast of the economic and social forces might include:

- Likely prospects for continued population growth.
- Customer willingness to increase or decrease their level of spending.

- Trends in employment and median income levels.
- Effects of shifts in attitudes toward automated bank services.

The results of forecasting and the identification of the assumptions are summarized in the environmental position report. Additionally, commentary about the probabilistic nature of forecasts and the degree of confidence warranted should be included.

Environmental Position Report

The environmental position report brings together the important findings from environmental scanning. The report should contain summaries developed throughout this phase of strategic planning. Suggested contents of such a report include the following:

- Economic Report
- Regulatory Considerations
- Social Trends
- Technological Considerations
- Competitive Profiles
- Market Profile
- Customer Profiles
- Threats
- Opportunities
- Forecasts and Assumptions Analysis

Conclusion

The benefits of environmental scanning efforts are not simply the preparation of a more credible financial forecast or the mere tracking of cause into effect. The benefits are derived from the realization that a certain environmental factor can impinge directly on the bank to the point of threatening its very survival. In such cases, identification, careful monitoring and contingency planning are in order.

In summary, environmental scanning involves:

- Identification of factors in the external environment that will affect the bank during the planning horizon.

- Identification and understanding of the strategic success factors that will make or break the bank.

- Analysis, evaluation and forecasts of how the environment will affect the bank.

- Identification of business threats and market opportunities.

This chapter has positioned both the remote and proximity environments as critical to effective strategies. The criticalness is not intended to imply, though, that each factor in the environment is equally important or equally applicable to all strategic planning efforts. Neither has an organization of environmental forces meant to imply that the various areas of force are unrelated. The reality of a complex environment is such that conceptualization is necessary to assist management to think clearly.

4 INTERNAL ANALYSIS AND POSITION ASSESSMENT

"It's not that they can't solve the problem, it's that they can't see the problem."

... G. K. Chesterton

Simultaneous with scanning the external environment, you must also look inside the bank to assess its current position, capabilities, strengths and weaknesses. Your goal is to learn as much as possible about your own bank so that you can answer such questions as:

- What do we do better than our competitors?
- What strengths are not being marketed effectively?
- Which weaknesses should be remedied?
- Which services should be discontinued?
- What is the financial health of the bank?
- Does the bank have the necessary human/financial resources?
- What is the bank's ability to defend itself from environmental threats?
- Are the bank's operations efficient and cost effective?

The pursuit of opportunities should consider internal strengths and capabilities as well as external opportunities. For example, profitable opportunities might be forecasted for U.S. firms trading with the Pacific Basin countries (e.g., China, Japan, etc.). This trading activity represents an opportunity for banks located near these firms, especially in major West Coast ports. However, unless the bank has some expertise in international trading and foreign currency operations, it would likely be inappropriate to pursue a

Pacific Basin marketing strategy before developing an internal capability.

The benefit of internal analysis is that it:

- Serves as a foundation for objectives, goals and strategies.
- Identifies the bank's strengths and weaknesses.
- Brings together divergent internal perspectives.
- Presents a comprehensive picture of the bank.

Failure to adequately understand the bank's capabilities by assessing only its current situation could result in either unachievable strategies or strategies that do not fully exploit the bank's strengths. In either case, the bank's full profit potential is not realized.

Realistic self-examination is difficult and often unpleasant. It involves reviewing existing practices, challenging traditions and looking at the bank critically. It is generally considered to be stressful and more difficult than external scanning. As a result, bankers often slight internal analysis in favor of more extensive external analysis. A better solution would be to have a structured approach with clearly defined activities that would make this examination easier, thereby reducing the tendency to slight it.

The flowchart in Figure 4-1 illustrates our approach to conducting an internal analysis and position assessment. The assessment starts with developing and documenting a comprehensive picture of the bank. We need to know how well the bank performs those tasks essential to being a bank. The next identifies and evaluates the bank's strengths and weaknesses. This step is followed by matching the bank's strengths and weaknesses to the environmental opportunities and threats. This provides the final basis for developing an internal position report that summarizes the bank's current situation and becomes the foundation for objectives, goals and strategies.

Analyze Current Position

The purpose of analyzing the bank's current situation is to develop and document a comprehensive understanding of the

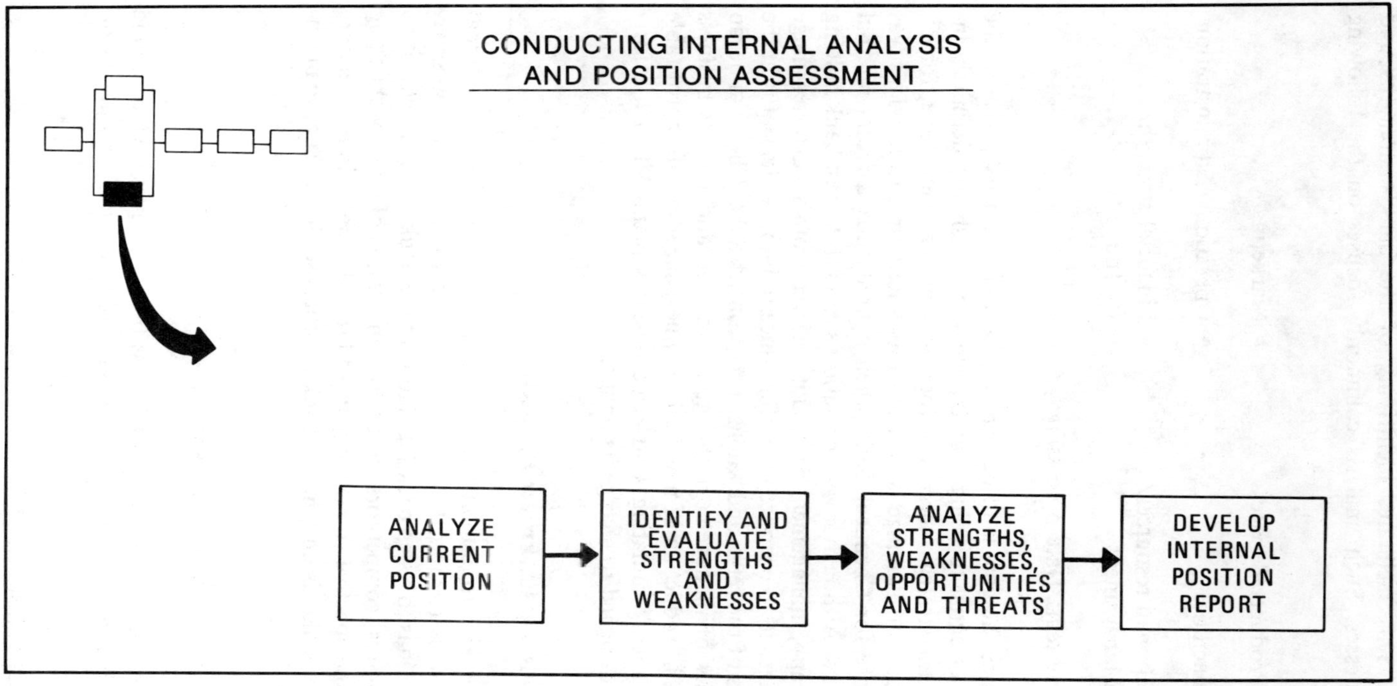
CONDUCTING INTERNAL ANALYSIS
AND POSITION ASSESSMENT
ANALYZE CURRENT POSITION
IDENTIFY AND EVALUATE STRENGTHS AND WEAKNESSES
ANALYZE STRENGTHS, WEAKNESSES, OPPORTUNITIES AND THREATS
DEVELOP INTERNAL POSITION REPORT

FIGURE 4-1

bank. This facilitates identifying of the bank's strengths and weaknesses. Such analysis commonly focuses on the following areas:

- Products/Services
- Marketing
- Facilities
- Operations/Administration
- Human resources/ Management
- Financial strength/ Profitability
- Systems/Data processing

Since the goal is to determine how well the bank performs the tasks essential to being a bank, the analysis should definitely include the strategic success factors. A bank may determine, for example, that its image is critical to its long-term success. This was the case for Chemical Bank when it undertook a recent internal analysis. Although it was the nation's seventh-largest bank holding company, management decided it suffered from a lackluster image and needed to energize its performance to improve its status in the minds of the retail and wholesale customers alike. Chemical began a series of management changes, reconfigurations of its business units, introduction of new business lines, shedding of unprofitable ones and formulating a strategic business plan. All such efforts were designed to change its image.

Establishing the Proper Perspective

The key to establishing the proper perspective for internal analysis is to view the bank from the perspective of an outsider. The idea is to "step back" and look at the bank from the eyes of its customers, competitors, regulators and shareholders. By changing your perspective you often gain additional insights into the nature of the bank. Examining the bank as others see it is the key to meaningful internal analysis.

Techniques for Internal Analysis

The following subsections discuss the techniques we have found valuable in conducting an internal analysis. These techniques include:

- Checklists

- Interviews
- Questionnaires
- Financial analysis
- Merger and acquisition valuation.

Checklists... We use checklists for each area to ensure a thorough analysis. Figure 4-2 illustrates a *portion* of a checklist for analyzing the bank's human resources. It highlights some of the major factors that should be examined when assessing human resources. Figure 4-3 illustrates a *portion* of another checklist, this one designed to cover products and services. Without the structure provided by the checklists, internal analysis could likely overemphasize some factors and totally exclude others.

CURRENT POSITION CHECKLIST

FACTORS TO BE EXAMINED IN ANALYZING HUMAN RESOURCES

- Management
  - Depth
  - Experiences
  - Effectiveness
  - Expertise
  - Interests
  - Capabilities and skills
- Compensation
- Performance measurement and incentives
- Attitudes
- Staff experiences and prior education
- Turnover and absenteeism
- Personnel advancement
- Hiring and advancement practices
- Technical competence

FIGURE 4-2

CURRENT POSITION CHECKLIST

FACTORS TO BE EXAMINED IN ANALYZING PRODUCTS/SERVICES

I. Overall View of Products/Services

- Product differentiation
- Advertising costs
- Special promotions
- Overall image
- Market coverage
- Etc.

II. For Each Product/Service

- Market share
- Product's image
- Performance
- Projected future performance - increasing/decreasing
- Volume
- Revenues, costs, and profits
- Products standing with key customers
- Uniqueness
- Pricing strategy
- Effectiveness of advertising
- Etc.

FIGURE 4-3

Interviews and Questionnaires... Much of the data needed in internal analysis will be available directly from financial statements, marketing surveys, personnel studies and other internally documented material. Also information can be generated by interviewing bank personnel, customers and regulators.

For interviews we have found that questionnaires are quite helpful. They force the interviewer into thinking ahead of time exactly what he wants to know and to structure his questions accordingly. Figure 4-4 is a portion of an interview questionnaire we have used to gather data on human resources.

INTERNAL ANALYSIS:

HUMAN RESOURCES AND MANAGEMENT DEVELOPMENT QUESTIONNAIRE

1. Are the critical functions staffed with well-qualified people?
2. Will there be special personnel needs - - (short or long term)?
3. What are the plans to respond to skill needs or technical obsolescence?
4. Will there by an excess of manpower in some functional areas? Can excess people be retrained for other positions within the organization?
5. Are successful and proven management personnel available to carry out plans or does everything depend upon one key person? What happens if this person is not available for an extended period of time?
6. Is there an adequate blend of experience?
7. Are there cohesive lines of authority and communication? Do all parts of an organization work closely together? Is there an integrated approach to all major problems?
8. Are the ranks frozen, with initiative stifled, and the imaginative and skilled employees frustrated because there is nowhere to go? Have development plans been established for key managers and high potential employees?
9. What is the strategy for filling key positions? Can internal development meet requirements or will outside hiring be required?
10. Is the compensation plan being administered so as to attract and retain top quality personnel?

FIGURE 4-4

Financial Analysis... Analyzing financial strengths and weaknesses requires a quantitative perspective. The approach is illustrated in Figure 4-5. For selected key performance measures the

MOUNT ST. HELEN COMMUNITY BANK
FINANCIAL PERFORMANCE ANALYSIS

	1983	1983 Comparative Bank Date (comparable asset base)	
	1983	**Average**	**High Performance***
Profitability			
1. Return on average assets	.29	.63	1.28
2. Return on equity	4.29	10.61	14.12
Asset and Liability Management			
3. Interest income (tax equivalent/average assets)	11.67	12.32	12.72
4. Interest expense/average assets	6.62	7.45	7.51
5. Net interest income/average assets	5.05	4.87	5.21
6. Earning assets/total assets	82.87	86.87	86.38
7. Gross loans/deposits	77.19	66.56	54.84
8. DDA/deposits	20.10	21.40	19.40
9. Cash and treasuries/DDA	88.70	79.79	86.26
Operating Efficiency			
10. Operating expense/assets	5.72	4.40	3.87
a. Salary & Employee Benefits	2.82	2.20	2.10
b. Occupancy & Furniture	.99	.62	.49
c. Provision for Loan Losses	.17	.36	.21
d. Other Expenses	1.74	1.22	1.06
11. Payroll expense per employee	$ 16,352	$ 17,350	$ 18,645
12. Assets per employee	$590,007	$735,532	$918,950
Revenue Enhancement			
13. Loan income/gross loans	16.47	19.51	24.85
14. Noninterest income/average assets	1.33	.91	1.08
Credit Quality and Leverage			
15. Net charge off/average loans	.06	.56	.30
16. Reserve/net loans	.06	.10	.10
17. Equity/average assets	6.96	8.44	9.79
Growth			
18. Loan growth	16.20	.16	(.16)
19. Deposit growth	2.15	1.91	4.62
20. Equity growth	.64	2.28	10.87

*Top six out of twenty-four in return on average assets

FIGURE 4-5

bank is compared to industry statistics. Take care not to compare your bank solely to the industry averages. This approach includes comparisons of the bank to selected competitors and those institutions similar in nature who are the "high performers" in the banking industry.

Merger and Acquisition Valuation... Another technique we recommend is to determine the economic value of the bank from the perspective of another institution considering acquiring your bank. Look at yourself critically from the perspective of an acquirer. This technique tends to be very objective since a purchaser would pay for strengths and discount for weaknesses.

This approach offers an additional advantage should you actually receive an offer from an acquiring institution. The board often does not have enough time to determine whether or not it is in the best interests of the institution to sell and if the price is acceptable. Emotions almost invariably prevail in these situations because facts surrounding the bank's economic valuation are not known. In effect, by going through this analysis in advance and establishing an economic value of the bank, both management and the board are better prepared to respond to any takeover attempts.

Evaluating Strengths and Weaknesses

The next major task in internal analysis and position assessment is the identification and evaluation of the bank's strengths and weaknesses. Because identification of relative strengths and weaknesses has been an integral part of both environmental scanning and analyzing the current position, we shall discuss their evaluation here.

The technique we have found most useful is for bankers to concentrate on identifying their *strongest competitive advantages* and their *strongest competitive disadvantages.* Your strongest competitive advantage is anything that favorably *distinguishes* your bank from its competitors in the *eyes of the customers.* Note, this is not how *you* perceive your strengths and weaknesses, but how your customers perceive them. Probable basis for competitive advantage or disadvantage would be such things as product, price, service, image, etc.

In evaluating strengths and weaknesses, we are mainly concerned with materiality and relevance. To accomplish this we need to organize and document them; identify those that need to be developed further; and see how the strengths and weaknesses relate to each other. We have found Figures 4-6 and 4-7 useful in evaluating strengths and weaknesses and in organizing them for use later in internal analysis process. Figure 4-6 compares the bank to each of its principal competitors. This kind of analysis reinforces whether a strength or weakness is truly genuine. Environmental Scanning should provide the information necessary for this competitive analysis. Figure 4-7 pulls the strengths and weaknesses together and organizes them into a single report. This report is useful as a first pass to see how they relate to each other.

Strengths, Weaknesses, Opportunities and Threats Analysis

The last task involves a matching of the bank's internal strengths and weaknesses with the environmental threats and opportunities. We refer to this effort as a strengths, weaknesses, opportunities and threats (SWOT) analysis. Since one of the primary purposes of strategic planning is to identify opportunities and threats and to make plans to exploit or avoid them, SWOT analysis is critical. Figure 4-8 illustrates this matching concept with a two by two matrix. As shown, opportunities in the external environment can be matched to either bank strengths and weaknesses. Likewise, environmental threats can similarly be matched.

There are several benefits of performing a SWOT analysis that warrant comment:

- Minimization of the risk that significant strengths and weaknesses or material opportunities and threats have been overlooked.

  In this sense a SWOT Analysis acts as an insurance policy by allowing you to approach internal analysis from two different perspectives (internal vs. external).

  For example, during internal analysis you may have identified a particular weakness in your bank. While evaluating that weakness you might discover a threat that you had not thought about before. Alternatively, you could have identified an opportunity while scanning the environment. Considering that opportunity may stimulate your thinking about a strength your bank has that had may not have been recognized during internal analysis.

ILLUSTRATIVE COMPETITIVE COMPARISON

Evaluation Criteria	Principal Competitors: Toledo National	Walbridge Federal	Maumee State	Our Bank	Comments
VI. Administration					
• Relation to Holding Company					
• Communications					
• Coordination of Actions					
•					
•					
VII. Human Resources					
• Competence					
• Compensation and Incentives					
• Employee Attitude					
• Staff Experience					
•					
•					
VIII. Management					
• Expertise and Competence					
• Commitment					
• Experience					
•					
•					
IX. Organizational Structure					
• Extent of Formalization					
• Role of Board					
• Strength of Executive Committee					
•					
•					
X. Communications					
• External with Community					
•					
•					
IX. Product Lines/Service					
• Degree of Innovation					
• Depth and Breadth					
•					

Evaluation Criteria	Principal Competitors: Toledo National	Walbridge Federal	Maumee State	Our Bank	Comments
I. Profitability					
• Deposit Growth Rate	1.5%	(1.0)%	3.0%	2.5%	Above average growth
• Return on Assets	.21%	.63%	1.28%	.29%	Below average
• Return on Equity	10.61%	8.31%	14.21%	4.29%	Very below average
•					
•					
II. Operations					
• Number of Branches	5	3	6	5	
• Location Convenience	Excellent	Adequate	Excellent	Good	
• Range of Service	Full	Limited	Full	Selected	
• Branch Autonomy	Very homogeneous	Homogeneous	More autonomous	Less autonomous	
• Correspondent Relationships	Good	OK	Excellent	Satisfactory	
•					
•					
III. Marketing					
• Image	Market leaders	Close to community	Solid image	Good, But detoriorating	
• Delivery Systems	Extensive autom.	Antiquated	Under developed	Adequate	
• Pricing Policies	High, value added	...	...	More aggressive desc.	
• Depth of Services	Excellent	Good	OK	Very good	
•			Product package	Advertising campaign	
IV. Finance & Accounting					
• Item Processing					
• Relative Strength of Financial Function					
V. Data Processing					
• Method of Processing					
• Ability to Accommodate New Products					
• Degree of Strategic Support					
• Personnel					
•					
•					

FIGURE 4-6

BEVERLY HILLS NATIONAL BANK
INTERNAL ANALYSIS
KEY STRENGTHS AND WEAKNESSES
Marketing*

Issues	Selected Strategic Implications
Strengths	
• A full-time marketing director and staff assistant.	We enjoy a relatively good marketing effort over our competition.
• Comprehensive branch sales training programs supporting branch management.	
• Positive customer awareness of the bank's image as a progressive, innovative institution that caters to select clienteles.	
• Additional funds available for promotion.	Facilitates our aggressive advertising program.
Weaknesses	
• No market research function on bank's market or customer profiles.	We are vulnerable to market shifts, particularly to non-bank financial institutions.
• Only minimum product/services, cost/benefits information.	
• No product developments and a follow-the-leader mentality with respect to new services.	Could eventually adversely impact our image. Causes a constant reactive environment within the bank.
• No meaningful CIF to evaluate customer relationships or account profitability.	Certain profitable accounts could be getting less attention than deserved, making them more vulnerable to competition.
• No formal business development responsibility assigned to the branch managers for deposit acquisition and retention.	
• No formal marketing budget.	

*Adapted from "Strategic Planning for Future Bank Growth", by Metzer and Rau. *The Bankers Magazine*, July-August, 1982.

FIGURE 4-7

STRENGTHS/WEAKNESSES AND OPPORTUNITIES/THREATS MATRIX		
Internal Analysis of the Bank	External Analysis of the Environment	
	Opportunities	Threats
Strengths	• Most favorable area for bank strategies • Greatest likelihood for success • Bank is able to exploit opportunity	• Bank is able to counter threat • Declining long-term outlook
Weaknesses	• Area for turn around strategies • Area of future growth • Lost profits • Often requires commitment of resources • Expect new entrants into market	• Critical area of vulnerability • Requires immediate attention • Inability to counter threat • Exit, retrenchment, divestiture • Survival issues

FIGURE 4-8

- Identifies offsetting strengths and weaknesses not otherwise considered.

  What may be a strength (i.e., excellent industry penetration) could be a weakness in a situation where that industry is cyclical (i.e., steel, forest products, oil and gas, etc.)

- Facilitates the development of objectives and goals because as you do this match you start thinking about banking matters from different perspectives.

There is no single best way to prepare a SWOT analysis. There are several forms to accomplish this matching. One way to bridge the gap into goals, objectives and strategies is shown in Figure 4-9. This is a classic opportunities and threats driven SWOT analysis. We like this approach because it underscores the idea that bank strategy is driven by opportunities and threats. This illustration is key-word driven to put enough depth to build realistic goals, objectives and strategies.

OPPORTUNITIES AND THREATS DRIVEN SWOT ANALYSIS

	Strengths	Weaknesses	Implications
OPPORTUNITIES			
To Acquire Red Hill Federal	• Technically competent personnel • Existing ATM network • Inhouse data processing • Adequate capital	• Outdated systems	• May be too costly • Regulators may disapprove • Provides entry into new market etc.
THREATS			
Availability of Personnel	• Well developed, competitive salaries • Bonus and profit sharing program • Training program	• No formal approval system for new positions • Policy of promoting from within	• Cannot expand market base significantly without additional people

FIGURE 4-9

Figure 4-10 illustrates another approach to doing a SWOT analysis. As in the previous figure, this format is also opportunity or threat driven. For each opportunity, the bank's strengths are identified and the weaknesses documented, along with their implications. What distinguishes this format from the previous one is the specific inclusion of risks. For example, are there any threats that would void this as a meaningful opportunity? What is the likely competitor reaction to any given move that we would make? What is the materiality or relevance of this opportunity? At this point we are mainly concerned with identifying key points and to taking note of them. We'll go into more depth on their strategic implications in the next chapter.

OPPORTUNITY DRIVEN SWOT ANALYSIS

OPPORTUNITY: Provide brokerage services to existing customers.

- STRENGTHS
  - — Existing bank staff could sell service
  - — Branches are strategically located
  - — Existing customer base
  - — Anchor location in financial district of downtown
    etc.

- WEAKNESSES
  - — Lack of capital
  - — Lack management depth to supervise new equipment
  - — Lack experience in brokerage
    etc.

- IMPLICATIONS
  - — Must raise significant capital
  - — Reorganization of management responsibilites
  - — Hire expertise in brokerage
  - — Remodel existing facilities
  - — Additional systems required
    etc.

- RISKS
  - — Brokerage could become even more price competitive
  - — Market size unknown
  - — May not get immediate approval of license request
  - — Customer may reject service
  - — Current attractiveness could deteriorate in event of a bear market
    etc.

FIGURE 4-10

Figure 4-11 is still another example of a SWOT analysis. This illustrates a slightly different perspective. We are concerned with the environmental factors, their probability of occurrence, the time frame envisioned, the significance of each and the nature of their impact. To the extent possible, these factors are identified as either a threat or an opportunity. The bank's strengths and weaknesses are then indicated.

FACTOR DRIVEN SWOT ANALYSIS — ENVIRONMENTAL VIEW

Environmental Factors	Probability of Occurrence	Time Frame	Significance of Impact	Nature of Impact	Opportunity (O) or Threat (T)	Strengths	Weaknesses	Strategic Implications
• Trend toward purchasing over leasing	High	Current	High	Increased commercial lending	O	Strong customer base Industrial & high tech	Commercial loan dept. not perceived as "TOP" commercial service	Develop personnel expertise Market our commercial service
•								
•								
•								

FIGURE 4-11

FACTOR DRIVEN SWOT ANALYSIS — INTERNAL VIEW

Internal Factors	Importance to Bank	Importance to Market	Nature of Impact	Strengths (S) or Weakness (W)	Opportunities	Threats	Strategic Implications
•Capital position	High	Low	No funding for new products/ services Bank growth limited	W	Market could be good for selling stock or converti- ble debentures	Regulators may limit bank growth or force a shrinking of the institution	Raise capital through issuing new stock Could result in inappropriate visability of our capital problem within community Extensve cost in management time associated with any new security
•							
•							
•							

FIGURE 4-12

Figure 4-12 takes a similar approach except from an internal perspective rather than an environmental perspective. Hence internal factors are listed along the left-hand column. We then note the importance to the bank, the importance to the market and the nature of the force's impact. Each force is identified as a strength or a weakness and related to opportunities and threats. Finally, the strategic implications of each internal factor are identified.

As we mentioned in the beginning, there is no single best way to do a SWOT analysis. What is important is to bring different perspectives together so that you see new relationships and the strategic implications of those relationships. If your analysis is comprehensive, identifying objectives and goals and developing strategies will come easier. Many strategies are developed from working with the SWOT analysis because management begins to think within a broad structured framework.

Don't be too concerned if things don't tie into a neat package at this point. We have offered four different approaches that we have used or seen used because we are concerned that you get as much substance as possible out of this effort. Because this analysis will likely not remove all environmental uncertainty, questions may be left unanswered. There could be a number of ambiguities because there will be opportunities that are not backed up by either strengths or weaknesses. There will be strengths that do not obviously translate into opportunities. You must recognize there is nothing wrong with that.

Summary

The purpose of internal analysis and position assessment is to determine where the bank is now. You must know where you are now in order to map a strategy to get to where you want to go! The chances of you arriving at your final destination without knowledge of where you currently are is slim indeed.

Figure 4.12 gives a similar approach except from a functional perspective rather than an environmental perspective. Functional factors [illegible] ... importance to the ..., the importance to the ... and the ... of the ... figure is identified as a strength or weakness [illegible] components and [illegible]. Finally, [illegible] are identified.

As ... mentioned at the beginning, there is no simplest way to do a ... analysis [illegible] perspectives together [illegible] implications of these [illegible] comparisons [illegible] and [illegible] along with the SWOT analysis [illegible] a good structural framework.

[illegible]

Endnotes

[illegible]

5 MISSION, OBJECTIVES AND GOALS

"In the long run men hit only what they aim at."
... Thoreau

The objective of strategic planning is to develop strategies to enable the bank to profitably cope with an uncertain future. Central to accomplishing this objective is the establishment of the bank's mission and the development of realistic objectives and goals. This chapter elaborates on the discussion which began in Chapter 2 on these three elements.

A methodology is presented in Figure 5-1 to help you develop a reasoned response to anticipated future events, rather than a conditioned response to past or current situations. Inattention to mission, objectives and goals have caused many firms to misallocate resources, pursue conflicting strategies, overlook profitable opportunities and ignore significant business threats.

Defining the Business

The broadest choice you face as a banker is to define the "business" of your bank. Traditionally, the activities of banking were clearly defined, and hence, choices were limited. Today, however, the business of banking is not as easily identified. Banks are acquiring brokerage houses (e.g., BankAmerica's acquisition of Charles Schwab & Co.), establishing themselves as futures commission merchants (e.g., Continental Illinois National Bank & Trust Co. and NCNB) and entering the venture capital market (e.g., U.S. Bancorp). With nationwide banking just around the corner and with the current technological capability to connect every corner of this country to a single centralized automated delivery system, it has become not only important, but critical, to define your business.

At the macro level, your options include being a financial:

- Supermarket

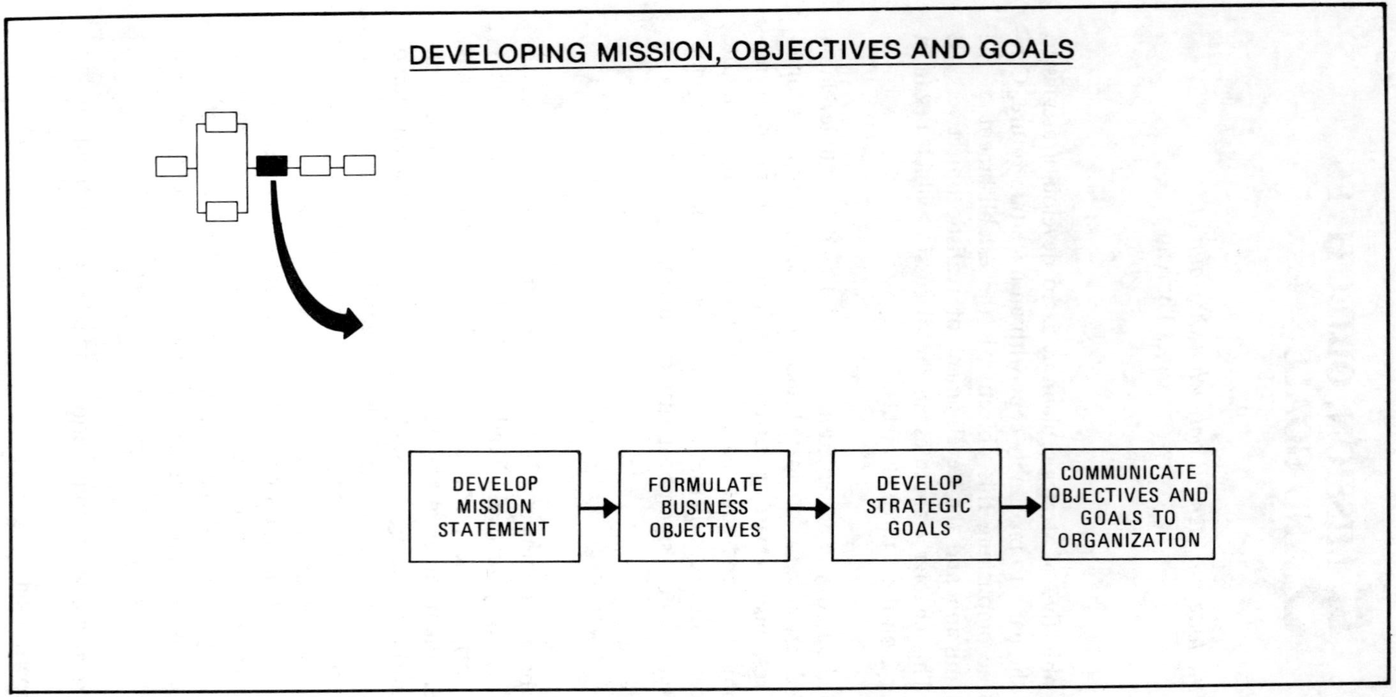
DEVELOPING MISSION, OBJECTIVES AND GOALS
DEVELOP MISSION STATEMENT
FORMULATE BUSINESS OBJECTIVES
DEVELOP STRATEGIC GOALS
COMMUNICATE OBJECTIVES AND GOALS TO ORGANIZATION

FIGURE 5-1

- Franchiser
- Non-Retailer
- Discounter
- Boutique

For example, Bankers Trust Co. of New York simply walked away from retail banking and by the early 1980s had turned itself into one of the nation's few pure wholesale banks. CitiCorp, through the use of state-of-the-art technology, and Bank of America, with its extensive full service branch network, see their purpose as serving the low cost nationwide retail market. Morgan Guaranty has defined its purpose to be serving the needs of the nation's top "blue-chip" corporations, a boutique for the bluest of the blue. In each case, these and other banks are not only defining their businesses differently, but also chosing different approaches to the following issues:

- Markets to be served
- Geographic areas to be served
- Products/services to be provided
- Facilities (delivery systems) to be used
- Technology
- Social responsibility
- Image

Defining the business is synonymous with finalizing the preliminary mission. As we discussed in Chapter 2, a mission statement indicates what management is really trying to accomplish. It entails finding a market need which will support a profitable business. It reflects the CEO's beliefs, values, priorities and aspirations for the bank. It also describes the image he wishes the bank to project. When the mission is articulated, it communicates the desired long-term direction of the bank by indicating the basic services to be provided, primary markets to be served and the means of serving those markets. The mission statement serves as a reference point for orientating the efforts of the bank. During the process of formulating the mission, you begin to identify the issues which you will need to focus on during strategy development (Chapter 6).

There are no simple answers to the question of "How do I develop a mission?" However, several techniques we have found helpful include:

- Developing alternative missions.
- Openly discussing the mission with your management.
- Reviewing it periodically for continued validity and focus.

In addition, we have used the following questions to evaluate a bank's mission statement:

- Does it have a tone which conveys the desired image?
- Does it encourage unanimity of purpose within the bank and SBUs?
- Does it serve as a rallying point for the organization?
- Does it provide guidance to the planning committee and managers to resolve resource allocation problems, priorities, etc.?
- Is it a reasonable basis for building a strategic plan?
- Is it explicit enough to facilitate its translation into objectives, goals and strategies?
- Is it internally consistent?
- Does it recognize outsiders' views?

Although choosing the mission is among the most highly unstructured decisions a banker can make, it should be through explicit rather than implicit choice. Too often, bankers assume that their mission is either obvious or implied from current bank actions. They may be reluctant to explicitly go on record since this may:

- Only serve to highlight existing uncertainty and indecision.
- Stifle creativity or limit scope of activities.
- Become a standard to judge their own performance.

The fundamental challenge with documenting a mission is to chart a course between something so broad that it is a statement on motherhood to something so specific that it becomes a bank objective. Too broad a statement does not provide the guidance that your people need. As a result, they are likely to neglect important areas, fail to recognize opportunities and not anticipate developing threats. At worst, various managers may even develop conflicting strategies; in effect, putting the bank into competition with itself.

On the other hand, if the mission is too narrowly defined managers could become too absorbed in achieving that mission while excluding other activities. Consequently, many very profitable opportunities may be ignored because they are "outside" the mission. Companies in such diverse industries as railroads, movies, dry cleaning and food service are well aware of the costs of too narrow a mission.

Figure 5-2 illustrates sample mission statements for three hypothetical banks. They represent different approaches and each has a different tone or variation in its focus.

Developing and evaluating a mission clarifies the bank's reason for existing. There are no right or wrong ways to prepare a mission, but it certainly should be openly discussed so that it can serve as a rally point for those who identify with that mission. Lastly, the mission provides overall direction to the efforts of the bank. It doesn't matter how carefully you climb each rung of a ladder if, when you reach the top, you find it leaning against the wrong building.

Expectations of Stakeholders

A stakeholder is a group of individuals who place relatively

REPRESENTATIVE MISSION STATEMENTS

JACKSON COUNTY FEDERAL BANK

Our business purpose is to optimize long range return to our shareholders by building an institution that focuses solely on the financial needs of our local community.

We believe this course requires diversification of our product line to enable us to accommodate all the financial affairs of our customers. Their convenience has and will remain of utmost importance. And to this end we pledge to offer the best customer service in our market area.

We recognize the valued contributions of our employees and to them we pledge our full sense of respect and support and an environment that enables and encourages their highest sense of job satisfaction.

FIRST FEDERAL BANK OF OMAHA

First Federal of Omaha will seek to optimize benefits to its stockholders by creating a financial institution that is more responsive than its competitors to the needs of the community that it serves. It will anticipate the financial needs of our customers and work hard to create new opportunities to put the community's resources to work locally.

First Federal believes that in order to be truly a service-oriented institution, it must strive to balance service to customers with the essential goal of survival as a strong financial institution. This necessitates selecting services on the basis of their contribution to First Federal's overall health.

First Federal of Omaha will achieve its goal of an optimum level of service consistent with maintaining its position as a strong community institution through the cooperative efforts of management, employees and owners.

SECURITY EASTERN BANK

Our primary mission is to capitalize upon the major industry forces of change, with the primary purpose of building an institution that will not only survive, but remain a profitable one in the future.

This acomplishment of our business mission involves:

- Expansion within our basic geographic territory by adding new market areas and increasing penetration in areas we currently serve.
- Extending into altogether new geographic areas as regulations allow.
- Broadening our range of financial products and services.
- Strengthening our competitive position at every opportunity.

We believe that the successful financial institution of the future will be the one that offers a wide range of services over a broad geographic territory. And we intend to be that type of financial institution.

FIGURE 5-2

homogeneous demands on the bank. Figure 5-3 identifies the major stakeholders for a commercial bank.

The demands of stakeholders should be specifically considered when determining and evaluating the bank's mission, objectives and goals. For example, the mission should reflect the stockholder's expectations for profits, dividends, growth and marketability.

Stakeholders can exert significant pressures on the operations of the bank and management should be sensitive to them when determining and evaluating mission, objectives and goals.

A California based financial institution illustrates how stakeholders exert pressures upon management. The regulators wanted to shrink the size of the institution because of inadequate

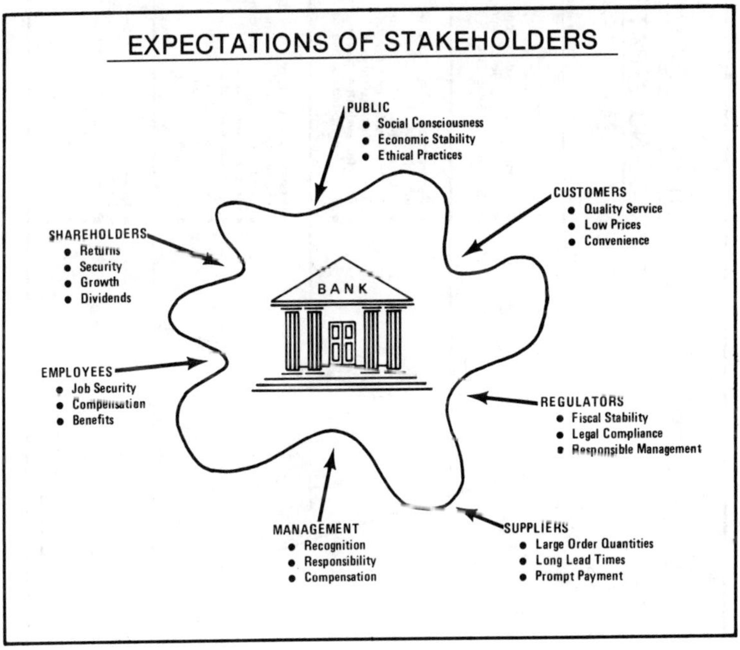

FIGURE 5-3

capital. The only viable option they identified was for the institution to sell off a major location that had a highly visible presence in the community. Their proposed action set off a storm of protests. Employees were concerned with job security. Customers did not

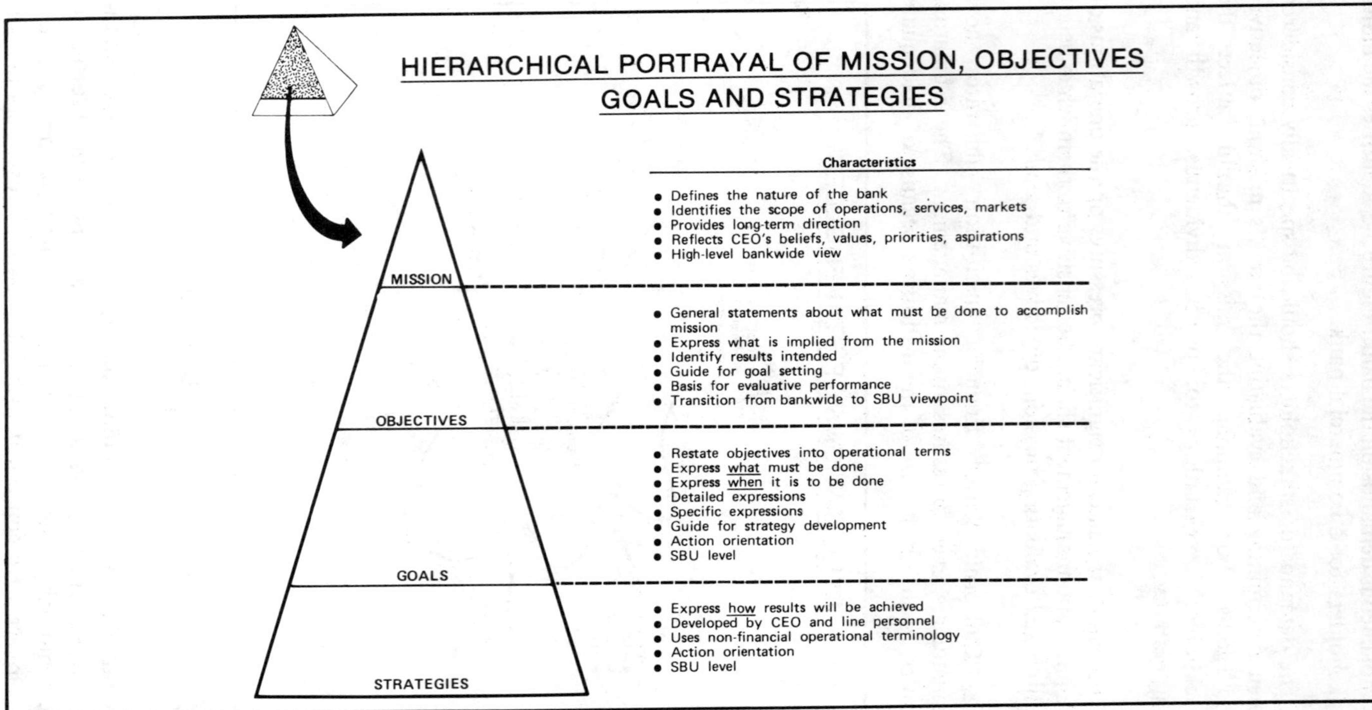
HIERARCHICAL PORTRAYAL OF MISSION, OBJECTIVES
GOALS AND STRATEGIES
Characteristics
MISSION
• Defines the nature of the bank
• Identifies the scope of operations, services, markets
• Provides long-term direction
• Reflects CEO's beliefs, values, priorities, aspirations
• High-level bankwide view
OBJECTIVES
• General statements about what must be done to accomplish mission
• Express what is implied from the mission
• Identify results intended
• Guide for goal setting
• Basis for evaluative performance
• Transition from bankwide to SBU viewpoint
GOALS
• Restate objectives into operational terms
• Express what must be done
• Express when it is to be done
• Detailed expressions
• Specific expressions
• Guide for strategy development
• Action orientation
• SBU level
STRATEGIES
• Express how results will be achieved
• Developed by CEO and line personnel
• Uses non-financial operational terminology
• Action orientation
• SBU level

FIGURE 5-4

want the location closed because it would mean a loss of service and convenience. Management was concerned that such a visible shrinkage would be capitalized upon by their competitors and would risk a run on deposits. The shareholders were concerned with the future economic value of the smaller entity. The regulators wanted fiscal stability. The board had to balance these pressures long enough to allow management time to work out a meaningful solution.

Objectives

Before discussing how to establish and evaluate the bank's objectives, it may be worthwhile to review the conceptual model of mission, objectives, goals and strategies. Figure 5-4 shows the critical elements of a strategic plan and identifies the key characteristics of each.

Since objectives were defined and illustrated in Chapter 2, we are principally concerned here with:

- Elaborating on the nature and purpose of objectives.
- Identifying current issues.
- Discussing criteria for evaluating objectives.
- Communicating the objectives.

The broad directional statements contained in the mission must be translated into more concrete terms, thus making action possible. The first step in this translation is to develop business objectives which support the mission. This can be accomplished by taking key phrases or messages from the mission statement and translating it into generalized statements which express more specifically the desired future position of the bank.

Typically, we see banks develop objectives for the following areas:

- Economic value
- Image
- Revenues and profits
- Productivity
- Diversification
- Management development

- Return on assets
- Net interest margin
- Market share
- Product/service development
- Social responsibility
- Capital adequacy
- Facilities and delivery systems.
- Technology

Objectives should be established in each area where the bank faces a meaningful business issue. For example, objectives in the area of capital adequacy should address the critical issues on capital formation facing the bank. Figure 5-5 provides a representative list of current issues which should be reflected in the bank's objectives.

The criteria useful in evaluating existing or proposed objectives are enumerated in Figure 5-6. This list also serves to further define the nature of objectives. It is presented in no particular order and is not mutually exclusive.

We have found that communicating objectives which have an *action* orientation is easier and more effective. This action orientation is accomplished not only by the ideas inherent in the statements but also by their phrasing. Using active rather than passive verbs creates the impression of actionable dynamic ideas. As simple as it sounds, it makes a noticeable difference as can be seen by a single example:

- Our market share of consumer loan *shall be increased.* (passive)
- *Increase* our market share of consumer loans. (active)

Stating objectives in such an active manner enhances the impact and motivational nature of your strategic plan.

In the vocabulary of the business world there are a good deal of semantic problems with the terms "objectives" and "goals." Some organizations do not differentiate between the two and use them interchangeably, while others which distinguish between objectives and goals, may give them the opposite meaning that we have here. That is not important. What is important is that the bank give each term a specific meaning and make sure that everyone understands the bank's definition of objectives and goals.

REPRESENTATIVE CURRENT ISSUES DRIVING THE FORMATION OF BANK STRATEGY*

- What kind of changes should be anticipated in the deposit base?
- What will be the source of future bank capital?
- What is the impact of the shifting customer attitudes on the future of financial institutions?
- What are the new product trends on the lending side of the bank?
- What new products and services should be anticipated?
- What will happen with respect to the competition from the Federal Reserve Board?
- Will regulations bring new competition?
- What is the impact of deregulation and reregulation of Reg D, Reg Q, the McFadden Act, Bank Holding Company Act and Douglas Amendment?
- How will small and mid-sized banks be able to differentiate themselves?
- What should our posture be toward the prospects of being acquired or acquiring other institutions?
- What kind of network do we want to establish with other banks and what impact will that have on our traditional correspondent relationship?
- What is the impact of such technology as debit cards, ACHs, home banking, ATMs and the like?
- What kind of human resource implications are there with regards to the capabilities of the chief executive and his management team?

---

*Adapted from "New Dimensions in Banking: Managing the Strategic Position," published by Arthur Andersen and Company and the Bank Administration Institute.

FIGURE 5-5

CRITERIA FOR EVALUATING OBJECTIVES*

Suitable...	The objective must make a contribution to move the bank in the direction of its mission.
Feasible...	It should be possible to achieve objectives in light of the external and internal scanning.
Acceptable...	Objectives are more likely achievable if they reflect the values and priorities of the responsible personnel.
Flexible...	It should be possible to modify the objective for unseen contingencies.
Motivating...	If attainment is out of reach or too easily achieved, then little motivational power exists. Objectives should be aggressive, but not out of reach.
Understandable...	Language should be simple and unambiguous. Objectives should be understandable by those responsible for them.
Linkage...	Objectives should be internally consistent and mutually support the mission. Accomplishment of objectives should insure progress toward accomplishment of mission; therefore, they should cover all areas critical to the bank's mission.

*Adapted from **Strategic Planning,** by George A. Steiner, The Free Press, New York, 1979.

FIGURE 5-6

Strategic Goals

Strategic goals take the development of bank objectives one step further down the planning pyramid. They are specific expressions describing what must be done to achieve the objectives. Goals do not express *how* the objectives would be accomplished, this is left to strategies; they do express *what* must be done and by *when.*

The characteristics of effective goals begin with those identified in Figure 5-6 for objectives. In addition, goals should also be:

- Specific
- Quantified (measurable)
- Dated

For example, a bank's objective may be to "use high technology electronic banking to gain increases in the retail market." One goal this objective may spawn could be "to introduce on-line teller terminals in all branches by the end of 1985." This goal is specific, quantified and dated.

Goals should also be linked to the performance measurement and reward systems and strike a balance between long-term and short-term outlooks. Although goals should be quantified, this can be overdone. The compulsion to quantify everything, under the assumption that if it is a number suddenly uncertainty disappears, should be avoided. Quantify when it needs to be and where it makes sense.

An overview of methods to use in setting bank goals (and objectives) is presented in Figure 5-7. As shown, numerous approaches exist, from simple extrapolations of past performance to sophisticated econometric models using economic and industry trends.

To illustrate the planning hierarchy more completely, Figure 5-8 presents a portion of a bank's mission translated into strategies for one organizational unit.

Communication

The mission, objectives, and goals must be communicated to those individuals responsible for strategy development. This report could result in the first serious challenge to the definitions of strategic business units, economic assumptions, mission, objectives and goals. For example, as lower level bank management find

METHODS TO EMPLOY IN SETTING OBJECTIVES & GOALS*

Past performance...	Assume that past trends will continue into the future.
Trend adjusted for future forces...	Adjust past performance trend for forces identified in external and internal scanning.
Industry trend and market share...	Use expected market share of projected total industry trend.
Resource use...	Identify resources available and determine their best use.
Negotiation...	Objectives and the result of negotiations between top and middle managers.
Top management dictated...	Top management's decision with or without analysis.
Iteration with strategy...	Going from mission to strategy is a repetitive process.
Results of SWOT analysis...	Identified through analysis of strengths, weaknesses, threats and opportunities.
Implied by mission...	Translation of mission statements into more operational terms.
From strategies...	Identify strategy first and then determine objective necessary to justify that strategy.

*Adapted from **Strategic Planning,** by George H. Steiner, The Free Press, New York, 1979.

FIGURE 5-7

themselves responsible for developing strategies, they may question the validity of the assumptions being used or the appropriateness of the mission, objectives or goals.

ILLUSTRATION OF MISSION TO STRATEGY DEVELOPMENT

MISSION:	• The primary mission of the Great Western Bank is to maximize the long-term value of the Bank to its owners.
OBJECTIVE:	• Provide competitive Trust products to support Bank growth.
GOAL:	• Increase the book value of trust assets 25% annually.
STRATEGIES:	• Study the feasibility of expanding corporate pension plan products to include Keoghs, IRA's, profit sharing plans, money contribution programs, etc. • Expand staffing to support growth by hiring an experienced pension plan trust officer. • Establish and implement an effective trust marketing program. • Upgrade the computer system to support more competitive trust services.

FIGURE 5-8

This situation can be partly avoided by maintaining good channels of communication throughout and beyond the initial planning process. Also, encouraging participation by more bank management personnel at appropriate points along the way helps create the sense that the plan is "their plan" and will lessen the natural resistance to change.

Summary

Mission, objectives and goals are the most important and yet least understood components of the strategic plan. Although the terms are common in the vocabulary of most bankers, there are countless instances where banks have lost their sense of mission, misallocated resources or sought conflicting objectives.

This chapter has tried to put these three key elements into a banking context to provide the proper perspective about their nature and purpose and to offer guidance about how to develop, evaluate and communicate them.

6 STRATEGY FORMULATION

"Take care to get what you like or you will be forced to like what you get."

... George Bernard Shaw

Formulating strategy is one of the most interesting and challenging aspects of strategic planning. The essence is to relate the bank to its environment. Efforts to this point have concentrated on *where* you want your bank to go and *what* you want it to accomplish. Now you need to create strategies suited to achieving your mission, objectives and goals. This strikes at the very heart of strategic planning.

Strategy formulation is important in the planning process because it lays out *how* the bank is going to accomplish its goals. Strategies are maps. Without a clear detailed map to direct the bank, it is unlikely that you will make any meaningful progress.

Additionally, the process of formulating strategies also produces other benefits:

- It allows the bank to determine inadequacies in the internal and external analyses.

- It facilitates testing of the practicality of the bank's objectives and goals.

The process of strategy formulation consists of four principal elements: identification of strategic issues, development of alternative strategies, evaluation of each alternative, and selection from among the alternatives. This process is illustrated in more detail in Figure 6-1.

Formulating strategy begins with *verifying the basic strategic framework*. At the macro level, is your basic strategic thrust going to be as a full service commercial bank, a large discounter of retail

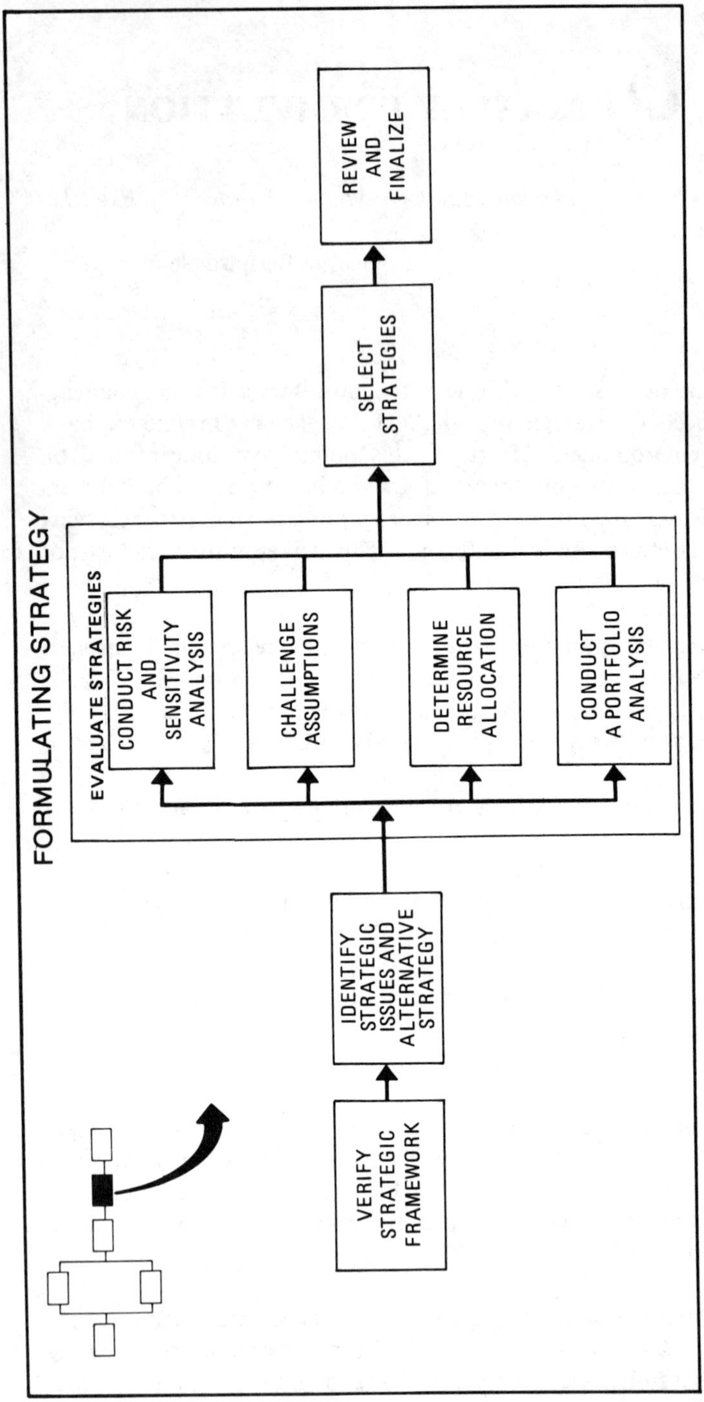
FORMULATING STRATEGY
VERIFY STRATEGIC FRAMEWORK
IDENTIFY STRATEGIC ISSUES AND ALTERNATIVE STRATEGY
EVALUATE STRATEGIES
CONDUCT RISK AND SENSITIVITY ANALYSIS
CHALLENGE ASSUMPTIONS
DETERMINE RESOURCE ALLOCATION
CONDUCT A PORTFOLIO ANALYSIS
SELECT STRATEGIES
REVIEW AND FINALIZE

FIGURE 6-1

services or a specialist in a particular geographic area? Why? Does the selected framework make the most business sense? Is the rationale for this choice on solid enough ground to withstand an aggressive challenge?

With a basic thrust in hand, the major strategic issues confronting the bank must be identified, defined and addressed. This will involve the generation and evaluation of alternative strategies. Such strategic issues should have surfaced by this point through consideration given to the strategic success factors, competitive profiling, and the development of the SWOT analysis.

Dealing with key strategic issues involves the generation and evaluation of alternative strategies. We like to evaluate alternative strategies from a number of different perspectives:

- Risk.

  Strategy formation by its very nature is risk-taking decision making. Thus, the idea is to better understand the risk and manage it rationally rather than haphazardly.

- Resource requirements.

  Evaluating resource requirements includes determining what resources are required to carry out the strategies and evaluating their availability and cost.

- Sensitivity to assumptions made.

  Strategies are based on assumptions such as economic growth, interest rate and buying patterns. To the extent certain assumptions are critical to strategy accomplishment, they should be scrutinized even more closely. This would include looking at the sensitivity of the strategy to changes in the assumptions and the probability of the assumption materializing as planned.

- Extent it fits in with other bank plans.

  The bank can accept some individual strategies with higher risk if they are balanced by others less risky. An examination of all strategies could identify situations where the risks are cumulative instead of off-setting, exposing the bank to an unacceptable risk level.

Basic Strategic Framework

There are several basic strategies banks can use to create a defendable position within their industry. The best strategy for any given bank depends, of course, on its unique circumstances. No single strategic approach will work equally well for all banks. Instead, it has to be tailored to fit both the bank's competitive environment and internal capabilities. As a generalization, however, Harvard Business Professor Michael Porter has grouped the various approaches into three "generic" categories. These generic competitive strategies are:

- Cost leadership
- Differentiation
- Focus

In addition, he expressed that a firm can rarely successfully pursue more than one of these strategies simultaneously because each requires a total organizational commitment.

A *cost leadership strategy* is an attempt to be the lowest cost producer in the market. Outside the banking industry, this strategy is evident in Stanley hand tools, Briggs & Stranton engines, Texas Instruments calculators and Black and Decker power tools. These firms have established themselves as the low cost producers in their industry by:

- Aggressive construction of cost effective delivery systems.
- Vigorous pursuit of cost reductions.
- Tight control of overhead.
- Avoidance of marginal customers.

From a banking perspective, to be the low cost producer requires a large capital investment in state-of-the-art processing and delivery systems and close supervision over processing activities. CitiCorp, for example, has clearly chosen this strategy. It is creating barriers to competitive entry by committing so much capital into electronic delivery systems that few will be able to match their investment and offer cheaper retail banking.

A *differentiation strategy* attempts to create the perception that the firm is unique. Traditionally this differentiation is along one of the following dimensions:

- Design
- Image
- Technology
- Service
- Distribution network

For example, Mercedes Benz automobiles has clearly differentiated itself from much of the competition through design, construction and image. In electric ranges Jenn-Aire differentiated itself through exclusive features. In each of these approaches, the firms have been successful in creating the perception that they are different enough from the competition to warrant higher prices.

First Interstate Bank's strategy is to differentiate itself in the spring of 1982 by initiating the first franchise program in the history of U.S. banking. Under the program the franchised bank adopts the First Interstate name and purchases a set of products and services. While the bank retains local ownership and management, it has access to the technological advances of First Interstate's ATM network without the associated development costs. This has allowed the bank to further initiate the expansion of its name and services geographically and establish clear differentiation in the eyes of its customers. Banker's Trust of New York's concentration on wholesale banking is another example of a bank pursuing such a differentiation strategy.

A *focus strategy* implies that the firm is targeting a particular buyer/customer, product line or geographic segment. The concept is to serve this particular segment better than anyone else. Kentucky Fried Chicken has exploited this strategy to the point of stressing it in their advertising campaigns — "We do only one thing and we do it right." Walt Disney Productions has very successfully focused their efforts on the younger movie audiences by tailoring a product especially suited for their audiences' tastes.

Morgan Guaranty has focused on the bluest of the blue chip corporations. Oregon Bank stresses its geographic focus through the name of the bank (i.e., an Oregon bank can best serve the needs of the people in Oregon). Another example of a focus strategy is a California financial institution that expressly advertises that it serves the banking needs of the gay community of San Francisco.

The dilemma facing today's banker is to choose the best strategy. Should their strategy be one of cost leadership, differentiation or focus? Historically, many banks have tried to do all three. It is common, even today, to find community banks trying to be the low cost producer of a wide range of services, each focused on different market segments, while at the same time trying to differentiate itself from its competitors by numerous branches, personal service, ATMs and image campaigns.

Today, however, it is unlikely that a smaller bank could realistically pursue a strategy of cost leadership. This strategy entails a capital investment beyond its capabilities. In fact, each banker should carefully review your existing strategies and the proposed strategies to make sure you are not inadvertently pursuing a cost leadership strategy without realizing it. In the long term it is highly unlikely that the smaller institutions can compete with CitiCorp, Bank of America, Sears, American Express or Merrill Lynch solely on price.

If we rule out cost leadership, this leaves differentiation and focus as the broad strategic options for most institutions to consider. As a long-term strategy, focus can be highly risky. For example, if your focus is personal banking for individuals who have net worths over $250,000, and you are profitable, the natural tendency is for competition to develop. Your profitable segment or niche will dissipate. You must then be prepared to differentiate yourself from your new competition. The timing of this is crucial to continued profitability. Therefore, focus is most effective as a short-term strategy.

Consequently, differentiation may be the only long-term strategy viable for the small to medium-sized bank involved in anything other than a very small and isolated market.

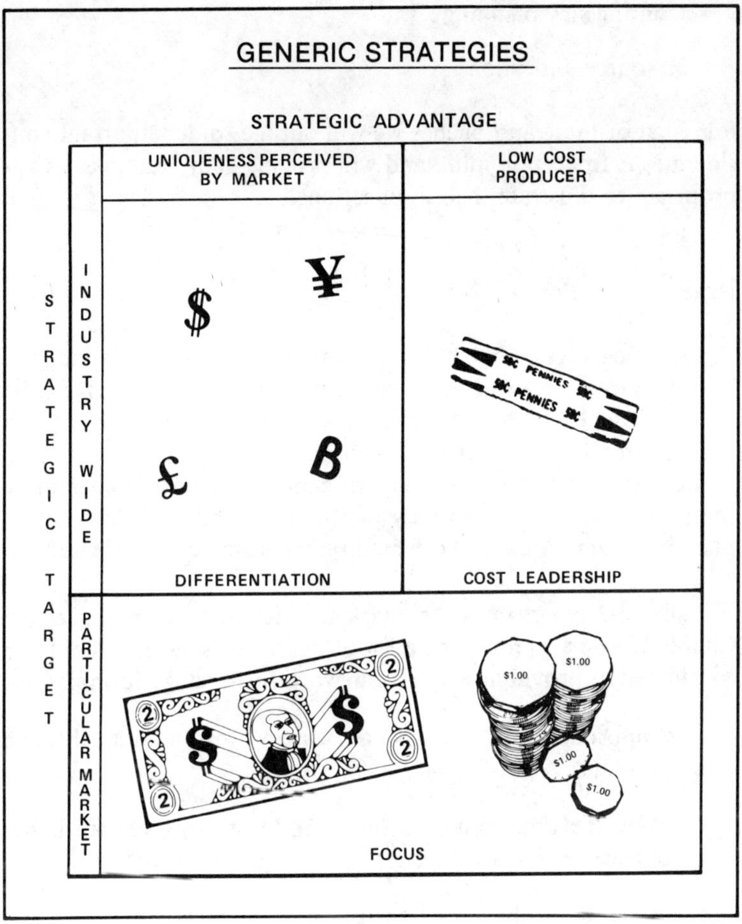

FIGURE 6 2

Strategy Evaluation Approaches

The remainder of this chapter develops a number of evaluation approaches. The major topics are as follows:

- Issues orientation
- Role of portfolio analysis
- Risk/Sensitivity analysis
- Challenging assumptions

- Contingency planning
- Resource allocation

For each of these approaches we will outline some important considerations to keep in mind and will provide bank examples as appropriate to illustrate their applications.

Issues Orientation

Strategic issues are the broad critical areas the bank must address in the strategic plan in order to ensure success. Focusing on the critical issues helps the bank concentrate on effective strategic planning and minimizes the risk of the process slipping into operational or budgeting matters. Issue identification and resolution require the involvement and creativity of the CEO and the full strategic planning team. An issues-oriented plan is also action-oriented.

Figure 6-3 enumerates the characteristics of strategic issues. In Chapter 5, we also provided a list of possible issues that should be considered as providing some framework for strategy formulation.

Our approach for addressing strategy formulation through strategic issues is as follows:

- Verify the importance of the issue by making certain it has the necessary characteristics of a key business matter.
- Define the problem or issue as explicitly as possible.
- Develop alternative strategies and outline the major considerations associated with each.
- Select the strategy for dealing with the issue.

We think this process is probably best portrayed by a case example. Figure 6-4 illustrates how one community bank dealt with the capital adequacy issue in its strategy formulation.

Role of Portfolio Analysis

Portfolio analysis as it relates to bank strategic planning is analogous to the portfolio techniques applied in the Investment or

CHARACTERISTICS OF STRATEGIC ISSUES

- Strategic issues are **future oriented.**
  Based on management's anticipation of future events.

- Strategic issues usually have **multi-business unit consequences.**
  Rarely is a strategic issue confined to a single business unit.

- Strategic issues may cause **major shifts** in responsibilities and **restructuring** of business units.
  Emphasis should be on a coordinated response.

- Strategic issues are **externally sourced.**
  Strategic issues come from the environment.

- Strategic issues will likely impact the **long-term prosperity** of the bank.
  Strategic decisions typically commit the bank for long periods of time with significant future cost implications.

- Strategic issues involve the **commitment** of large amounts of resources.
  This requires the careful consideration of the long-term impact.

- Strategic issues require **top management attention.**
  Their broad perspective is imperative since they have the authority to allocate the necessary resources.

- Strategic issues may result in **redefinition of mission** or business purpose.
  Some strategic issues are so significant that they may even result in changing the basic strategic thrust of the bank.

FIGURE 6-3

Trust Department to manage a collection of securities. Portfolio analysis refers to considering the bank (or its holding company) as a collection of business units.

The basic concept of portfolio analysis applied to banking is quite simple:

- The bank (or holding company) is viewed as a portfolio of business units, products or services.

(continued on page 116)

CAPITAL ADEQUACY — DRAFT POSITION PAPER

ADIRONDACK COMMUNITY BANK

Importance of Capital Adequacy

There are several reasons for our bank's concerns regarding capital adequacy. These reasons are:

- To protect depositors and other creditors from unexpected losses.
- To provide funds for building and other non-earning assets.
- To conform to the requirements of supervisory authorities.

However, because of the financial leverage that is provided by our use of non-capital sources of funds, we must balance meeting regulatory and creditor/depositor safety demands with the ROI demands of our bank's stockholders. Because of these diverse forces to be reconciled, the purpose of capital adequacy is twofold:

- Protect the persons outside our shareholder group who have an interest in our bank.
- Maximize shareholder return and simply maintain the bank's existence as a viable economic entity.

Capital Adequacy Defined

As we and the regulatory bodies have found out, determination of adequate capital triggers a complex debate because of the imprecise definition of the term "capital adequacy" and the requirement to exercise a considerable degree of judgment.

In 1981 the Federal Reserve Board and the Comptroller of the Currency issued capital adequacy guidelines that are being used by these agencies in assessing the capital of our bank as well as others. In implementing this capital program, the agencies are using two principle capital measurements. These ratios are:

- Primary capital to total assets.
- Total capital to total assets.

FIGURE 6-4

Primary capital consists of:

- Common stock.
- Capital surplus.
- Undivided profits.
- Reserves for contingencies and other capital reserves.
- Mandatory convertible instruments.
- Allowance for possible loan losses.

Total capital includes:

- Primary capital components.
- Limited life preferred stock.
- Qualifying subordinated notes and debentures.

The capital to assets ratios established as guidelines for our bank are 6% to 7%.

Overall Bank Strategies Available

There are essentially three strategies that our bank can pursue in seeking to improve capital adequacy. These strategies are:

- Generate capital internally through retained earnings.
- Seek external capital funding sources through the issuance of additional equity instruments.
- Reduce or limit the growth of the bank's asset base.

Internal Generation Strategy

Generating capital internally can be done by:

- Increasing net income by pursuing an aggressive profit improvement program.
- Reducing dividend payout.

Since there are only essentially two options for increasing capital through generating capital internally, suffice to say that our options are somewhat limited in this strategy particularly in today's economically troubled times.

FIGURE 6-4 (Continued)

External Generation Strategies

Seeking external sources for generating additional capital offer substantially more but complex options. These options are:

- Issue more common stock.
- Issue preferred stock.
- Issue qualified subordinated debt.
- Issue convertible securities.
- Institute an employee stock ownership trust.
- Issue deposit-stock certificates.
- Institute dividend reinvestment program.
- Offer stock option plans.

Let's consider 4 basic strategies for external sources:

Alternative #1: Issue additional common stock. Factors to consider include:

- The dilutive effects on current shareholders' return on equity.
- Decreased yield of stock issuance resulting from professional fees associated with the issuance.
- Increased regulatory scrutiny associated with public offerings.
- Pre-emptive rights of existing stockholders (under applicable state laws).
- Limited market for smaller banks' stock.
- Small bank control groups refusal to suffer a reduction in their interest percentage.

Alternative #2: Issue preferred stock. The factors to be considered are:

- Payment of preferred stock dividends comes from after tax earnings.
- Preferred stock is not a wide spread equity form in the banking industry.
- Regulatory authorities look on preferred stock as a much better alternative than debt.
- The preferred stock does not dilute common stockholders interest percentage but it may dilute earnings.

FIGURE 6-4 (Continued)

Alternative #3: Issue convertible securities (debt or preferred stock). The factors to be considered are much the same as those for preferred and common stock. Additional factors to be considered are:

- Convertible securities tend to be more complex financial instruments and more difficult for small banks to use.
- Convertible debt can usually be sold with significantly lower interest costs than straight debt because of the conversion privilege.
- The convertibility of the security may enhance its marketability.
- If the convertible security is issued with a call provision it provides the bank with a more flexible financing instrument.

Alternative #4: Issue subordinated debt. The factors to be considered are:

- Interest payments are from pre-tax earnings.
- There is little flexibility in cash management.
- Subordinated debt may not always be considered as part of capital reserves.
- The debt will eventually have to be paid off or refinanced.
- Lenders are becoming increasingly wary of accepting fixed-rate debt.

Bank Shrinkage Strategy

Reducing the asset base of our bank to improve our overall capital adequacy also has some important considerations:

- This would be the most acceptable approach to the regulators.
- Shrinkage would likely be very visable to our competitors and customers and could conceivably result in lower profitability due to loss of image.
- May believe the worst of our loan losses are behind us and we are poised for a turnaround in the future if we simply can buy some time.
- Attitudes of bank managers and employees would suffer further making it difficult to attract and keep management talent.

FIGURE 6-4 (Continued)

Recommended Position and Rationale

We have developed a recommended combination of approaches to deal with our capital adequacy situation. Although the financial dimensions are further evaluated under separate cover, the major components of our recommendation include:

- Halt all dividend payments.
- Launch immediately into a comprehensive and effective profit improvement program.
- Issue $3,000,000 in convertible debentures.

We believe that by doing everything possible internally has got to be our major emphasis for the long-term. The convertible debentures, on the other hand, should allow us to deal with our short-term problem.

FIGURE 6-4 (Continued)

- Senior management should evaluate SBU plans from a portfolio perspective.

- An analytical framework can be established to assist management in deciding how to allocate financial resources across its portfolio.

- The portfolio problem becomes one of balancing cash flows between business units in such a way that cash generated from low growth areas is used to support the cash requirements of high growth areas.

- Portfolio management provides a framework of viewing risk, cyclicality, market share, business attractiveness, etc.

Some of the more common portfolio management techniques include:

- Cash-flow analysis
- Risk analysis

- Equity-cash flow analysis
- Acquisition/divestiture analysis

Various consulting firms and business organizations have developed and packaged conceptual models and analytical techniques to assist management in this dimension of strategic management. Some of these, such as the Boston Consulting Group's growth share matrix, have been around for some time and have helped historically establish a conceptual identity to strategic planning. Figure 6-5 presents an imagery of these tools and Figure 6-6 discusses their generic advantages and disadvantages.

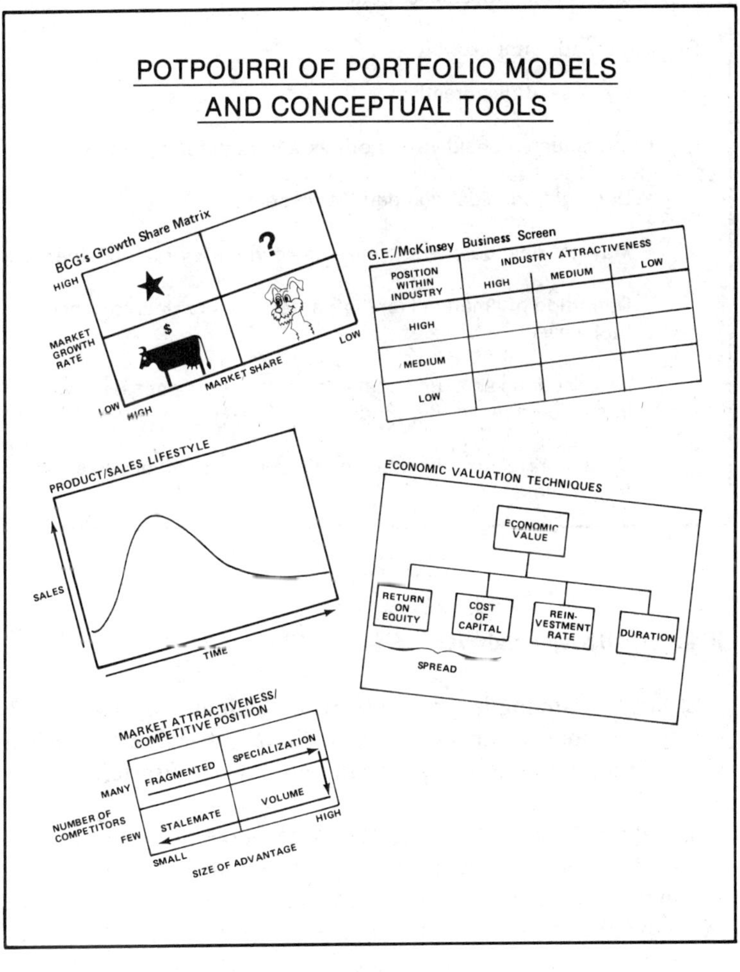

FIGURE 6-5

GENERAL ADVANTAGES AND DISADVANTAGES OF VARIOUS PORTFOLIO MODELS/TOOLS

Generic Advantages

- Usefulness of their simplicity in conceptualizing the business.
- Appropriate for mature established businesses.
- Facilitates the understanding of various roles and relationships among business units.

Generic Disadvantages

- Overuse stifles creativity.
- Inadequate consideration of risk and required investment.
- Does not consider competitive response.
- May not adequately recognize basic identity of the business.
- Definition of "market" (and other terms) is critical to conceptual view.
- Assumptions as to unit costs and output not necessarily valid in service or emerging product.
- Growth rate may be inadequate measure of business attractiveness.

FIGURE 6-6

Risk/Sensitivity Analysis

Strategic planning is not an effort to eliminate business risk. In reality, it is not even an attempt to minimize it because any such effort over a long period of time can only lead to disaster.

To take risks by committing present resources to future expectations is the essence of economic activity. While it is futile to try to eliminate risks, it is essential to choose the correct risks to take. Many believe the end result of successful strategic planning is the capacity to take on greater risks for this is the key way to improve performance.

For the bank to be successful it must understand and manage the risks it takes. Bank management must be able to choose rationally among its risk-taking alternatives rather than rely on tradition or intuition. Until recently, banking has existed to a large extent on guessing. Consider the recent trouble that First Pennsylvania and First Chicago got into when they guessed wrong on the direction of interest rates. Although both banks thought rates would go down, they continued to go up and stuck these institutions with a long-term portfolio. This resulted in significant losses and the removal of their chief executives.

There are two major approaches for considering risks. One involves a more conceptual view of the subject, the other a more quantitative perspective.

An illustrative conceptual discussion model for considering the risks of products and markets is shown in Figure 6-7. It highlights, for example, that taking a broader product line to existing markets is less risky than taking entirely new products to entirely new markets.

PRODUCT/MARKET RISK MODEL

PRODUCTS	MARKETS	
	EXISTING	NEW
EXISTING	LOWEST RISK	MORE RISK
NEW	MORE RISK	GREATEST RISK

FIGURE 6-7

Sensitivity analysis is the principal quantitative method for assessing strategy risk. Assumptions which are important to the bank's performance should be tested to determine the degree of sensitivity profits have to the options being considered. Figure 6-8 provides an example of how one small financial institution tested the criticality of its interest rate assumptions under one of its proposed strategies.

ILLUSTRATIVE INTEREST RATE SENSITIVITY ANALYSIS

	1985 $000		
	Base Case Strategy	Strategic Option 1	Strategic Option 2
A. Prime Rate	15%	15%	15%
Net Income (Loss)	($500)	($200)	$300
Loan Loss Reserves and Retained Earnings	$1,000	$1,400	$1,450
Total Assets	$42,000	$45,000	$46,500
B. Increase Prime Rate 1%	16%	16%	16%
Net Income (Loss)	($600)	($350)	$220
Loan Loss Reserves and Retained Earnings	$900	$1,250	$1,200
Total Assets	$40,000	$44,000	$45,500
C. Decrease Prime Rate 1%	14%	14%	14%
Net Income (Loss)	($375)	$-0-	$480
Loan Loss Reserves and Retained Earnings	$1,125	$1,600	$1,520
Total Assets	$41,000	$43,000	$46,000

FIGURE 6-8

Challenging Assumptions

We believe that challenging strategic planning assumptions is a necessary and critical aspect to successful strategy formulation and development. The success of the strategic plan can depend as much on the relevancy of the assumptions made as on the logical planning process itself.

Successful strategic planning requires that assumptions be identified and subjected to deliberate re-examination and reflection. Identification is the first step and often the most difficult because it is easy for bankers to overlook "hidden" assumptions by simply using past traditions as future givens.

In identifying and re-examining assumptions, the bank could employ a devil's advocate approach and subject particular strategic options to the most vigorous and forceful oppositions. While this will undoubtedly expose various assumptions, care must be taken that this approach is not so overly negative or destructive that no alternative options are revealed.

Another approach used to surface assumptions involves asking the questions "under what circumstances would this strategic option be optional?" This could be followed by outlining other possible strategies and asking the same questions.

A common assumption at many banks today is belief that geographic expansion is a function of establishing full service branches. Little consideration has been given to automated tellers as alternatives to human ones or the possibility of branches with greatly reduced hours or services in selected market areas. Many say that Bank of America's failure to challenge their assumptions on branch banking in California is an excellent case in point. Only recently did Bank of America conclude that its 1,000 plus branch network had too many full-service branches. It took escalating personnel and occupancy costs to force management to challenge such a traditional assumption as the invincibility of bricks and mortar.

Contingency Planning

Contingency plans specify actions that bank executives can pursue if a significant unanticipated event actually occurs. Contingency planning involves:

- Identification of key contingency events.
- Consideration of strategic implications of uncertain future events.
- Modification of objectives, goals and strategies to deal with such events.
- Establishment of confidence levels in business assumptions, forecasts and strategies.
- Identification of certain "trigger points" that would initiate predetermined contingency actions.

Because strategic planning is highly subjective in nature, there is a legitimate need to think through a series of "what if" questions to determine the effect of critical events on planned strategies. Sometimes contingency plans are developed after a bank completes its strategic plan rather than during the original process itself. Although we don't encourage this, what is important is that banks identify the need for contingency strategies early on and emphasize their development in a manner commensurate with the business risk involved.

The availability of financial models has greatly increased the bank executive's ability to do effective contingency planning by allowing him to quickly consider a wider range of implications of possible events and various scenarios to deal with them.

Resource Allocation

The allocation of resources is a fundamental choice in the formulation of strategy. Although scarce capital dollars is what typically comes to mind when discussing resource allocation, in reality there are numerous varieties of resources required to implement strategy:

- Money
- Facilities
- Personnel
- Management time

Resource allocations are often among the final decisions that are made in the development of a strategic plan. These allocations are made to business units, strategies and programs and frequently involve some of the toughest judgement calls.

The newer techniques relating to the creation of economic value have been particularly effective in assisting management to allocate business resources. We are firm believers in allocating resources to bank business in a manner that maximizes the value received. This requires adopting a state of mind that capital resources, for example, should not be allocated "between" competing needs, but rather, "to" individual SBUs based on their ability to earn over and above their cost of capital.

Intelligent resource allocation involves:

- Avoiding strategies that are more diverse strategy than you can afford.
- Allowing for contingencies and considering timing.
- Considering management time and commitment as precious as an overabundance of available capital.

Review and Finalization of Bank Strategy

As the various bank strategies are brought together and organized into a coherent strategic framework, it is extremely critical that they be reviewed for completeness and consistency.

It constantly surprises us how frequently bank strategic plans do not function together. Consider two recent examples:

- The difficulty banks had in the months following their introduction and promotion of money-market accounts in lending out their new funds.
- How ATMs have been improperly marketed to the public. While spending money on advertising and hardware, banks kept disincentives in place by continuing to offer generally free teller service.

Bank strategies must in the final analysis be *explicit*. This facilitates:

- Easier allocation of resources.
- A basis for motivating bank employees.
- Transition of broader objectives and goals into operating plans and budgets.

With the completion of the bank's strategies, we can now turn our attention to finalization of the full strategic plan.

7 FINALIZING THE STRATEGIC PLAN

"It is a bad plan that admits of no modifications."
... Publilius Syrus

You may wonder why we are placing such emphasis on finalizing the strategic plan. We recognize that your most likely inclination is to begin immediately implementing the strategies you have worked so hard to develop. This is natural, especially in those banks where the CEO has created the proper "can-do" atmosphere. Our intention is not to dampen this interest, but to finalize the plan so that it can be effectively and efficiently implemented.

We have found that strategic plans that consist of loosely organized collections of such documents as mission statement, environmental and position reports, and statements of objectives, goals and strategies cannot be fully implemented. The plan must first be brought together in such a manner that it can be reviewed for completeness, style, format and consistency. This is necessary to establish a single integrated version of the plan. Otherwise, implementation will go in several conflicting directions at once because the employees have different views about what is included in the plan. Further, the plan needs to be organized so that it can be reviewed and approved by top management and the board of directors. This approval is important because it demonstrates their continued interest in the plan and their support for the efforts needed for implementation. Without this expression of continued support, the plan would be implemented in a piecemeal fashion and be ineffective as a management tool. Figure 7-1 illustrates our approach to finalizing the strategic plan.

Content of the Plan

Although what is actually included in the final plan is primarily a matter of personal choice, we have included two representative outlines of the contents of a strategic business plan. These are shown in Figures 7-2 and 7-3.

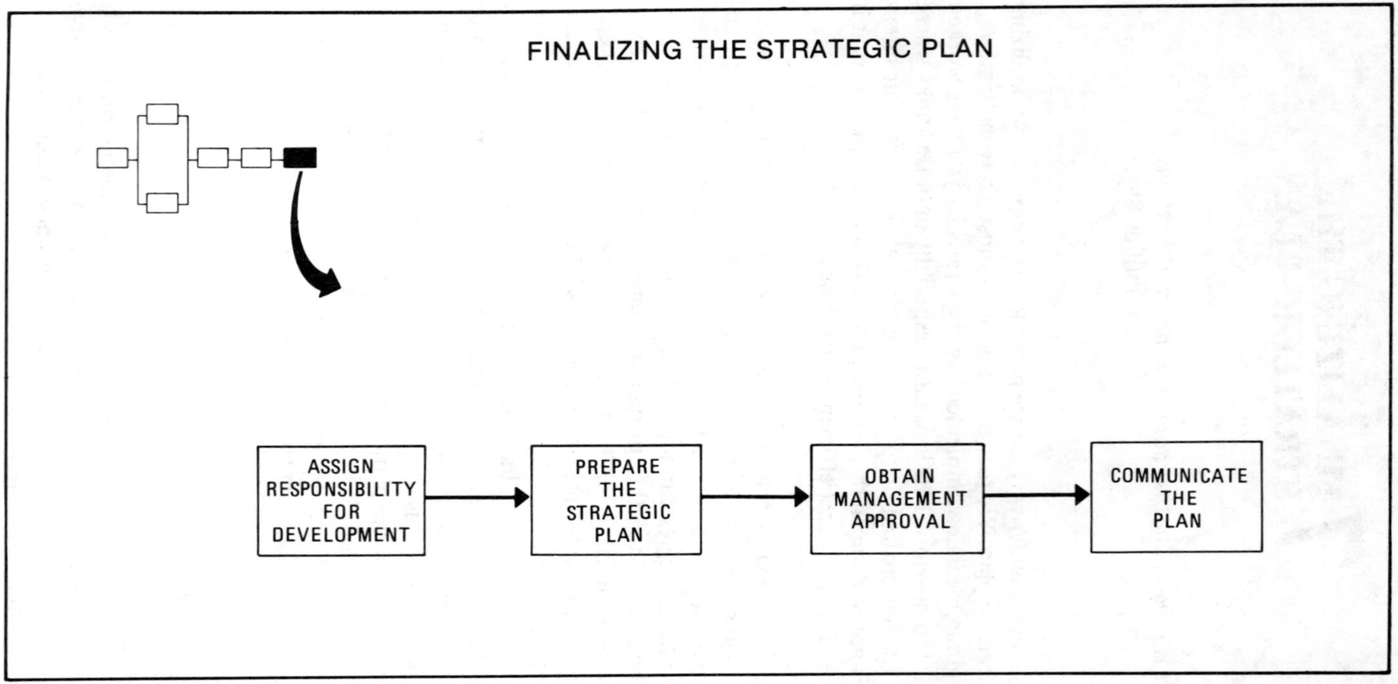
FINALIZING THE STRATEGIC PLAN
ASSIGN RESPONSIBILITY FOR DEVELOPMENT
PREPARE THE STRATEGIC PLAN
OBTAIN MANAGEMENT APPROVAL
COMMUNICATE THE PLAN

FIGURE 7-1

STRATEGIC BUSINESS PLAN
REPRESENTATIVE OUTLINE I

I. Introduction

II. Mission Statement

III. Objectives and Goals

IV. Assessment of Current Situation
   A. Historical Financial Performance
   B. Comparative Industry Statistics
   C. External Environment and Trends
   D. Internal Environment
   E. Summary Assessment

V. Financial Plan
   A. Introduction
   B. Review of Financial Plan
   C. Key Assumptions
   D. Summary of Results
   E. Financial Model

VI. Strategic Issues
   A. Introduction
   B. Buildings
   C. Data Processing Capability
   D. Branch Configuration
   E. Organization and Personnel
   F. Product Lines
   G. Customer Base

VII. Sensitivity Analysis
   A. Introduction
   B. Deposit Growth Sensitivity
   C. Interest Rate Sensitivity

VIII. Tactical Considerations
   A. Introduction
   B. Required Resources
   C. Implementation Plan

FIGURE 7-2

STRATEGIC BUSINESS PLAN REPRESENTATIVE OUTLINE II

I. Executive Summary

- Qualitative in Nature

II. Environmental Forecast

- Market Outlook
- Economic, Regulatory & Political Influencing
- Technology
- Identification and Evaluation of Key External Factors
- Forecast

III. Position Assessment

- Summary of Strengths and Weaknesses
- Detail Analysis
    - Products Mix and Quality
    - Personnel
    - Pricing
    - Systems
    - Financial
    - Market Positions
    - Etc.

IV. Business Plans

- Mission Statement
- Objectives and Goals
- Strategies

V. Financial Summaries

VI. Implementation

- Integration with Budget
- Monitoring Systems
- Responsibilities

FIGURE 7-3

The most important point is that the plan must be documented. Frequently, we have observed widespread agreement on the essence of the plan until it is put into writing. After people read the plan, the disagreements begin to surface as they realize the written plan is not what they thought they had approved. Writing is critical to bringing these disagreements to light, otherwise these people would have simultaneously been pursuing different directions.

The level of detail included in the finalized plan is an important consideration. A common pitfall is to use excessive detail to support each idea. This distracts the reader from the main point. Instead, a strategic plan should be lean, containing only enough detail to support the strategy and nothing more.

Consideration should be given to the style of presentation (e.g., writing style, format, appearance, etc.). A well organized coherent plan neatly presented emanates a sense of pride and credibility to the whole process. Some banks use special covers and tabs and printing prepared for the final plan to give it that polished professional look. The writing style should be logical and clear. Even the most complicated points, with some effort, can be simply stated. Also, the same writing style should be used throughout. Too many styles loosely strung together give the plan a disjointed appearance and distracts the reader from the coherent structure of the plan.

Reviewing and Approving the Plan

The initial review of the strategic plan is done by the planning staff. The primary purposes of this review are to consolidate the SBUs' plans at the corporate level and to identify inconsistencies. In addition, the staff should review for:

- Completeness
- Style
- Format
- Accuracy
- Detail

After the staff review, the plan should be circulated to key people in the bank. Their review serves two purposes. First, it maintains the involvement of the key people. It would be easy at this point to forget those people who are going to make or break the plan. You need to be sure the "key" people support the plan before it is approved by the board of directors. Second, their input is needed on both the quantitative and qualitative aspects of the plan. Their review would include the same criteria as the staff's review with one significant additional question: "Is the plan realistic and achievable?" Since these are operating personnel who will be held responsible for the outcome, they should have the opportunity to evaluate the final plan from this perspective.

The last level of review is by the CEO, the person with the broadest perspective. His review combines external and internal perspectives. His review should ask such questions as "does the plan take full advantage of the bank's opportunities?" Figure 7-4 presents a check list of questions we have found useful for a top level review of a strategic plan.

The final approval of the plan comes from the board of directors. The plan is formally presented and discussed by the CEO and executive managers.

Communicating the Plan

After the plan is approved by the board, it must be communicated. The primary issues involved in communicating the plan are distribution, content and confidentiality.

You must identify the audiences for distribution of the plan itself or selected information from the plan. The total audience consists of:

- Board of directors
- Top management
- Key employees
- Regulators
- Shareholders
- Customers

Having identified the audience, you must determine the depth of information appropriate for each. Most likely, the board and top

CHECKLIST FOR REVIEWING FINALIZED STRATEGIC PLAN

- Does the plan build on strengths?
- Does the plan correct or minimize weaknesses?
- Does the plan have a realistic appraisal of its markets, customers and competition?
- Are any strategies vulnerable to regulatory changes?
- Can the plan be understood by everyone who has the need to know?
- Does the plan balance risk and return?
- Does the plan conflict with existing strategies?
- Is the timing of the plan correct?
- Does the bank have the resources to achieve the plan?
- Are the resources available at acceptable cost?
- Is the organizational structure at the bank compatible with the plan?
- Is the plan acceptable to major stakeholders at the bank?
- Is the plan in conformance with moral and ethical codes of conduct applicable to the bank?
- Is the plan consistent with the bank's goals and objectives?
- Does the plan support the image that the bank wishes to portray?
- Is the plan realistic?

FIGURE 7-4

management would receive the complete plan along with supporting documentation. Key employees should receive the portion of the plan that relates to their activities. Regulators may require copies of the strategic plan or portions of it. Shareholders should receive information that indicates that the bank has completed its strategic plan and that efforts are underway to implement it. This may be a good time to announce to customers new services or other changes as a result of the strategic plan. In other words, use selected portions of the strategic plan to initiate new marketing efforts.

Disclosure of information to competitors is possibly a strategy in itself. For example, you may want your competition to know that you are going to leave some markets and pursue others. This may encourage them to pursue other markets and hence, avoid possible direct competition.

The last major issue is confidentiality. Much of the plan is extremely confidential. Several times in recent years major corporations have had their strategies or marketing plans stolen and disclosed publicly. A few years ago when Sears was redefining its business and making plans to enter the consumer financial market, a major newspaper in the Chicago area published the full text of the summary of Sear's long-range strategic plan. Similarly, McDonalds had its short-term highly confidential marketing plan (e.g., promotions, advertising, games, etc.) published in a marketing trade journal. Without proper control on copies of the plan, your strategic plan could also fall into the wrong hands.

In addition to the plan being leaked to outsiders, you must also consider the risk of your employees leaving your bank and going to work for your competition. To protect yourself, you should limit the distribution to employees on a "need-to-know" basis. This way you reduce your exposure if an employee leaves, yet you still have the employee participating in the plan.

Modifying the Plan

A good strategic plan must allow for modifications. However, a balance must be reached between excessive modifications and too few. The key is to know when to change course. Changing business conditions, personnel or capital may dictate a shift in emphasis in a plan already in motion. However, you do not want a document so flexible that it is so often modified that it provides no guidance. You must find a prudent middle ground. Types of events that could trigger modification include:

- Significant regulatory changes

- Major changes in competitor actions
- Sudden shifts in the economy
- Resignation of key individuals

To the extent possible, even these events should be anticipated up front in the planning process.

Planning in Subsequent Years

After the first year, the efforts to develop a good strategic plan in subsequent years are probably reduced and certainly refocused. Future efforts include "updating" such planning elements as external analysis, economic forecasts and position assessments. In fact, if the proper environment was established, these elements are updated throughout the year. Hence, when the plan is prepared they only need be reviewed and incorporated.

In addition, we suggest that in subsequent years you zero in on one particular aspect of the plan, develop it in depth that year, then go on to another topic next year. This way the overall strategic plan will continually improve. Areas for possible concentration include:

- Specific issues — Competition, technology, markets or customers.
- Specific planning processes — Monitoring progress, risk/sensitivity analysis, linking budgets to strategies, improving forecasting accuracy or enhancing incentive systems.

* * *

The plan itself is now finalized! At this point most books and articles on strategic planning end. They assume that the plan itself is the critical document and that implementation is, we guess, a secondary issue. We disagree! Strategic planning takes you only one-third of the way to the real goal — STRATEGIC MANAGEMENT.

STRATEGIC ACTION

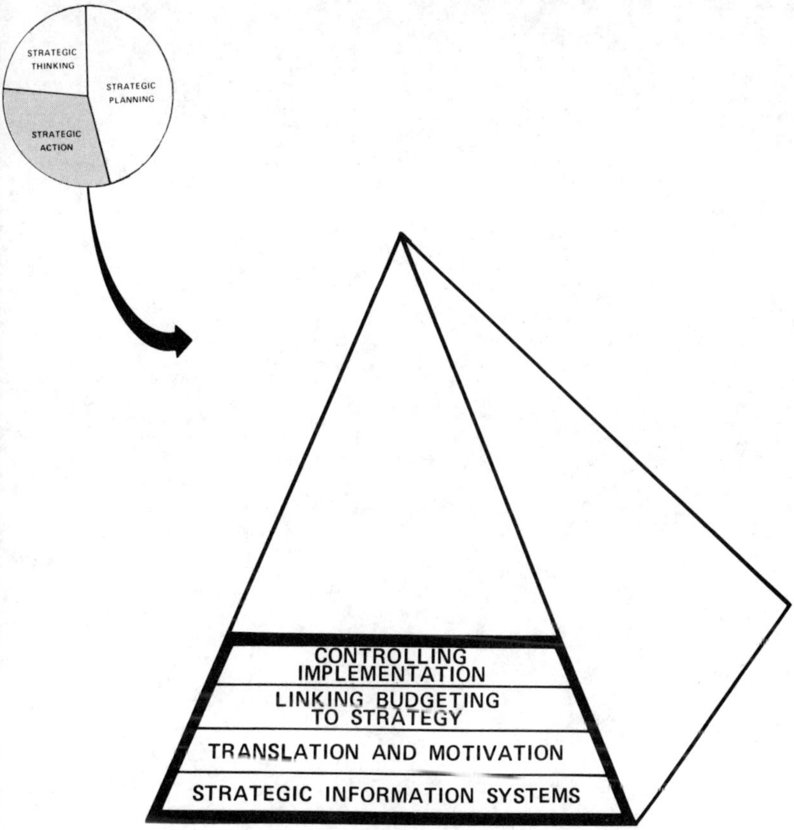

CHAPTERS 8-11

8 CONTROLLING STRATEGIC PLAN IMPLEMENTATION

"Our responsibility is not discharged by the announcement of virtuous ends."

... John F. Kennedy

With the strategic plan finalized, the first phase of strategic management has been completed. We now turn our attention to ... STRATEGIC ACTION. Chapters 8 - 11 examine the issues most critical to successfully translating strategies into actions:

- Controlling Implementation.
- Linking Budgeting to Strategy.
- Strategy Translation and Motivation.
- Strategic Information Systems.

Controlling implementation is the first major issue of strategic action. This chapter focuses on implementation techniques necessary to direct and control the bank's resources as it pursues its strategies. A plan has little effect if you do not or cannot put it into action. To illustrate, let us contrast two banks that have both put their first strategic plan together. A summary of their situation is shown in Figures 8-1 and 8-2.

Twin Cities National Bank had developed, by all standards, a "great" plan. Management thoroughly scanned the external environment for opportunities and threats and performed in depth competitive and customer analyses. They were able to identify its strengths and weaknesses. The plan included the development of strategies which fully exploited its opportunities and strengths. Strategies included programs for entry into the brokerage business and for marketing existing services/products. They created a new logo and adopted a slogan to fit with its new strategies. The plan was finalized and communicated to all key employees.

STRATEGY IMPLEMENTATION ILLUSTRATIVE EXAMPLE

BANK: **TWIN CITIES NATIONAL BANK**

BACKGROUND:
- Serves market size of 120,000 people.
- 40 years old.
- Stable management.
- Great branch locations and network.
- $100 million in assets.
- Historically profitable.
- Well respected community image.
- Only one major competitor.

NATURE OF STRATEGIC PLAN:
- GREAT
- Thoroughly scanned external environment.
- In depth competitive and customer analysis.
- Identified strengths and weaknesses.
- Fully exploited opportunities and strengths.
- Entering new businesses, i.e. brokerage.
- Unique marketing strategies for existing services/products.
- Enhanced image with new logo and slogan.
- Communicated to all key employees.

RESULTS AFTER 1 YEAR:
- No change from operations prior to strategic plan.
- Deteriorating employee morale.
- Implementation program misplaced.

FIGURE 8-1

STRATEGY IMPLEMENTATION
ILLUSTRATIVE EXAMPLE

BANK: **STATESMAN FEDERAL OF CHARLOTTESVILLE**

BACKGROUND:
- Serves a small but densely populated area of 200,000 people.
- 36 years old.
- $95 million in assets.
- Generally profitable, though incurred higher than expected loan losses last year.
- Experiencing tough competition from two nearby savings & loans.

NATURE OF STRATEGIC PLAN:
- GOOD
- Overview of external environment.
- Minimum information on internal strengths and weaknesses.
- More limited work done on external threats and opportunities.
- No image change or new services.
- Communicated to all key employees.

RESULTS AFTER 1 YEAR:
- Significant progress made on implementation.
- Ready to react when prime rate dropped.
- Key individuals monitoring competitors' moves.
- Morale level high.

FIGURE 8-2

Statesman Federal of Charlottesville, on the other hand, developed only a "good" plan. The bank had not scanned the external environment as thoroughly as had Twin Cities. Statesman

Federal had only marginal insights into the external threats and opportunities and into its internal strengths and weaknesses. The strategies it developed were good because they moved the bank toward its objectives, but did not fully exploit the potential as did Twin Cities'. The bank attempted no image modification and no new services. This plan was also finalized and communicated to all key employees.

One year later....

Twin Cities could not find its implementation program when someone asked to see it. The enthusiasm generated during strategy development had disappeared. When asked, bank management was hard pressed to report what progress had been made to put its strategic plan into action. Twin Cities had a "great" plan, but it was poorly implemented.

Statesman Federal, on the other hand, was ready to move into action when, for example, the prime rate dropped because it had identified strategies and assigned individuals to be ready for such a situation. The bank also had key individuals monitor each competitor's reaction to the execution of their strategies. Statesman Federal's plan was not "great," but it was well implemented.

Why was the situation so different in Charlottesville? Among other factors, Statesman Federal had:

- An adequate mechanism to deal with environmental changes quickly. Employees were alert to conditions that might alter the plan.

- Created major milestones to show employees' achievements during plan implementation that they could take pride in their success as a group and received recognition and visibility to the implementation.

- A CEO who sent periodic memos commending employees for their efforts. He let them know that the bank appreciated them.

- A management committee that met regularly to deal with implementation problems.

- Tied the strategic plan to the operating budget.

- Implementation work programs and timetables.

- Fixed responsbility for implementation.

- Provided coaching for employees to keep up enthusiasm during the implementation phase.

- Consistent follow-up efforts on work programs, schedules and dates for completion of tasks.

- Revised the strategic plan when it needed to be revised and stuck to it at other times.

We developed this contrast of two banks to introduce the significance of controlling plan implementation. Without control, there is little hope that the strategic plan will have any effect on the bank. We have concluded that a "good" plan properly implemented is much better than a "great" plan poorly implemented.

Implementation Strategy

Implementation is the process of transforming plans, strategies and policies into results. This phase of strategic management mobilizes the human, financial and capital resources to accomplish the bank's mission, objectives and goals. Hence, it requires careful attention to ensure the effective implementation of the bank's strategies.

The ideal approach should minimize unnecessary conflict between functional areas and should recognize the interdependencies between individual strategies. This requires the careful matching of plans to the bank's structure, people and environment. Properly done, successful implementation is not left to chance but managed like any other activity.

The key is to formulate a program to guide the implementation process. The program will serve as the basis for controlling the resources that have been committed.

The major techniques used to control strategy implementation include:

- Developing an implementation program.

- Designating responsibilities for each activity.
- Estimating start/stop dates and estimated work days.
- Identifying required resources and resource constraints.
- Establishing a system to monitor and report progress.

Some banks also make effective use of a critical path or PERT charts to further identify the interrelationship of implementation activities. We will not examine the use of these tools since they are well developed in other literature.

Implementation Program

An implementation program is a tool similar to the strategic planning work program discussed in Chapter 2. It is used to organize the bank's resources to convert the strategic plan into more specific activities and to monitor that these tasks are carried out.

You should have an implementation program for each strategy you develop. An advantage of preparing such programs is that you can determine the necessary steps to translate the strategy into action. In addition, the resources required for each strategy can be identified. Since assignment of responsibility is on a task or step basis, the implementation program is organized similarly. The time requirements for implementation — start/stop date, days required — are estimated along with benchmarks to monitor progress.

Then, the individual programs are gathered and considered as a whole to reveal a complete picture. In this way, conflicts can be identified and resolved. For example, if the bank does not have the personnel to do everything on a timely basis, then the strategies must be prioritized and the least important shifted to a slack period. Figure 8-3 illustrates an implementation program for a major strategy.

The individual strategies can be organized and presented in several ways:

- By start and completion dates.
- By responsible individuals.
- By resources required.

IMPLEMENTATION PROGRAM

STRATEGY: Achieve economies of scale to increase efficiency and profitability by combining operations of Gulf Coast National Bank and Gulf Bancshares Corp.

TASKS	RESPONSIBILITY	DATES START	DATES STOP	EST. EFFORT (WORK DAYS)	COMMENTS
FUNCTION: CORPORATE					
1. Streamline or centralize international and correspondent banking function	M. Gaines	June 10	Sept. 1	160	• Facilitates evaluation of total position with correspondents. • Aids in identifying "target" correspondent banks. • Eliminates duplication of efforts. • Aids development of expertise.
2. Establish consistent credit review	N. Oestreich	July 1	Aug. 1	50	• Provides consistent loan evaluation techniques. • Facilitates loan classifications on an overall comparable basis to identify total "classified" exposures.
3. Combine similar operations where applicable (i.e, leasing and mortgage loans)	R. Bartlett	June 15	Sept. 15	100	• Increases operational efficiencies. • Increases expertise. • Reduces overall training costs. • Matches volume wtih staffing.

FIGURE 8-3

TASKS	RESPONSIBILITY	DATES START	DATES STOP	EST. EFFORT (WORK DAYS)	COMMENTS
4. Establish one central wire transfer department for combined operations	M. Hulen	July 1	Aug. 1	65	• Reduces overlap of personnel. • Reduces exposure. • Increases efficiencies.
5. Establish procedures for loan accountability (by borrower and/or loan type) on an overall basis	D. Watne	July 1	Sept. 1	50	• Identifies total loan exposure (risk). • Shows loan concentrations. • Aids in establishing corporate lending objectives.
6. Establish centralized core group for pricing bank's services	N. Tang	June 15	July 1	10	• Develops innovative fee-based services to offset net interest margin pressure. • Provides consistency in approach and methodology. • Aids in monitoring of pricing policies.
7. Centralize loan processing activities (i.e., installment)	J. Bentley	July 15	Aug. 15	125	• Reduces number of personnel. • Reduces overhead costs.

FIGURE 8-3 (Continued)

TASKS	RESPONSIBILITY	DATES START	DATES STOP	EST. EFFORT (WORK DAYS)	COMMENTS
FUNCTION: RETAIL					
1. Centralize credit card functions	H. Rathe	June 1	Oct. 15	300	• Increases efficiencies. • Reduces exposure. • Reduces overlap of personnel. • Avoids duplication of resources.
2. Utilize combined deposit system	P. Turney	June 1	Oct. 15	55	• Avoids development costs. • Utilizes homogeneous system.
3. Synchronize ATM network	D. Murray	June 7	Aug. 1	140	• Good marketing tool. • Provides expanded customer service. • Increase fees.
4. Establish centralized core group for pricing banks' services	R. Mosley	June 15	July15	5	• Provides consistency of approach and methodology. • Aids in monitoring of pricing and few waiver policies. • Reduces duplication of efforts.
5. Develop profitability reporting system	D. Parker	June 1	Oct. 15	325	• Provides necessary information to management for determination of department, product and customer profitability.
6. Develop consistent branch manager incentive program	D Tang	June 1	Aug. 1	50	• Compensation based on employee performance.

FIGURE 8-3 (Continued)

Portraying the implementation by various dates allows you to quickly monitor progress. On a given date, you only have to scan the total program to see what should be just starting, what is in progress or should be completed. A planning bar chart, such as the one used in Chapter 2 (Figure 2-8), is one of the best means of showing this.

Organizing the programs by individual or other resources required serves two purposes. First, it shows an individual his total implementation responsibilities. Second, it reveals unrealistic demands on either an individual or resource that were not apparent on a strategy-by-strategy basis.

Management Responsibilities

While implementation programs are critical to successful implementation, they are not sufficient to ensure success. Every action must be done by an individual. This translates into leadership. The main leadership roles are assumed by the:

- CEO
- Executive management
- Executive planning committee
- Key operating managers

The CEO's role in strategy implementation does not differ significantly from his role in organizing and initiating strategic planning. He remains the dominant figure. His attitudes exert a major influence on the actions of others during implementation. His approach to change is very important as the bank shifts from the past to the future.

The importance of the CEO's role was very evident several years ago at Citizens & Southern National Bank of Georgia (C&S). The bank's financial affairs were in a total disarray. The Comptroller had recommended that C&S increase its loan loss provision by $15 million. The bank had to restate its 1977 earnings downward by $11 million and its stock price had fallen from a high of $26 to $4. By all accounts the bank was in trouble until a shake-up in top management brought in a new CEO. He immediately began delegating authority and holding people responsible for their assignments. He established a quarterly performance review system and stringent regulations about the use of capital. He developed a 5 year plan with an early warning system to detect deviations. Several years later, the bank had a much healthier financial picture. It was actively acquiring banks and was considered a serious competitor in the market.

Figure 8-4 outlines the major managerial responsibilities for strategy implementation.

MAJOR MANAGERIAL RESPONSIBILITIES IN IMPLEMENTING STRATEGIES*

1. Arrange the key tasks and sequences of steps to carry out policies and strategies required to achieve objectives.
2. Determine who is responsible for major specific tasks that must be discharged, steps that must be taken, and decisions that must be made.
3. Determine the major organizational structures within which implementation will take place, e.g., functional departments or decentralized product divisions.
4. Determine the resources (physical and human) necessary to implement policies and strategies and assure their availability when needed.
5. Determine types of performance required by organizational units and individuals and the dates when specific activities must be accomplished.
6. Determine the personal motivation and incentive systems to be employed.
7. Analyze the key interrelationships among people, organizational units and activities within units that require coordination and determine the appropriate systems to assure their proper condition.
8. Assure the proper degrees of participation in the formulation and operation of implementing systems and processes.
9. Establish appropriate information systems to assure accurate measurement of performance against standards so that corrective action can be taken when required.
10. Adopt training programs to develop the technical and managerial skills needed in implementation.
11. Assure that managerial leadership is effective in motivating and leading the organization in implementing policies and strategies in such a way as to achieve organizational ends in the most effective and efficient fashion.

*Adapted from Steiner, G.A. and Miner, J.B., **Management Policy and Strategy,** MacMillan Pub. Co. (New York, 1977).

FIGURE 8-4

Monitoring and Reporting Progress

Implementing strategic plans requires the same careful coordination as other critical bank activities. This implies periodic monitoring of progress, identifying activities which are not on schedule and taking steps to keep them on schedule (more help, etc.). It involves revising the timetable as necessary, holding firm when required and reporting progress to the executive planning committee.

Mid-Course Correction

From the beginning we have presented flowcharts and discussed strategic planning as if it occurred in a straight line, starting with mission and progressing directly through to actions. We know this is not realistic. When you get into implementation, you know the environment has changed since the strategies were originally selected. In some cases the changes are significant enough to warrant abandoning a strategy completely and pursuing one of its alternatives. To recognize when this change is necessary, you must have continually monitored the environment and related all significant changes back to the original strategies. Thus, your course is periodically being reevaluated, and receiving mid-course corrections, if you will, in response to unanticipated environmental changes.

Detecting environmental changes requires that you first identify those forces in the environment which warrant continuous monitoring. This would very likely include the strategic success factors previously discussed. Second, a system needs to be developed which will monitor these critical success factors. If the job was done as described in Chapter 3, then the mechanism to monitor these critical forces may already be in place. Lastly, a procedure should be in place to relate the environmental changes to the original strategies. This mechanism is commonly called a feedback loop. Feedback loops provide information to evaluate existing strategies, to evaluate the effectiveness of the planning system and to develop alternative strategies.

With an adequate feedback loop mechanism, the next issue involves determining how frequently the strategies should be revised. The system should not be so sensitive that it is constantly signalling for a change in strategy. You need to be alerted to those material and relevant changes in the environment that warrant consideration of strategic redirection. These changes could occur weekly in certain high risk matters, or most likely quarterly or annually in other major areas.

Conclusion

This chapter has discussed the critical importance of controlling strategy implementation. Although it may seem simple, we have observed not only how easy it is for great strategic plans to never get implemented, but also how difficult it is for management to maintain the enthusiasm that was generated during the initiation of the planning effort. This chapter has provided some guidance along both lines.

However, we do not want to overstate the case for implementation. Many of you have been inundated by the current morass of planning literature that says implementing strategy is everything. The literature wants you to believe that the real key to strategic planning is implementation. Our position is somewhat different. We view a major key to strategic planning is starting with a good plan. One reason there is so much attention being given to strategy implementation is that many strategic plans are so poorly developed that implementation is essentially impossible.

The next chapter links the shorter-term view of budgeting and annual planning to the longer-term view of strategic planning.

9 LINKING BUDGETING TO STRATEGY

"Don't bite my finger — look where it is pointing."
... Warren S. McCulloch

No one denies that good budgeting and profit planning can make valuable contributions to the bank. A good budget improves managerial communications and provides key personnel with a better understanding of operations. It serves as a guide for action and sets standards for performance. It also aids in improving profits by providing a quantitative basis for monitoring and controlling performance. It is the link between the strategy and the daily decision maker.

Since profit planning techniques and the mechanisms of the annual budgeting process have been around for many years, it is not our intent to address such basics here. Rather, we will focus on answering such questions as follows:

- How does budgeting relate to strategic planning?
- How can the two be linked together more effectively?

This chapter will discuss these two questions along with the problems commonly encountered when you attempt to link the budget to the strategic plan. We will also offer some guidance on how to effect the necessary linking.

Contrasting Budgeting with Strategic Planning

The results the bank seeks to achieve within a one-year period are specified in its annual budget or profit plan. These results are commonly restated on a monthly or quarterly basis so that periodic monitoring of actual performance can take place. The budget is very specific and detailed about what is expected from each department. As a result, it is organized so that it parallels the organizational structure of the bank, usually departmentally and geographically.

The strategic plan, on the other hand, takes a longer, less detailed view of what the bank seeks to accomplish. It is most likely expressed in less quantified terms without being divided into departmental segments. Contrasted to the annual plan, the strategic plan is organized around the business units.

The perspective of annual budgeting is efficiency — doing things right, whereas the perspective of strategic planning is effectiveness — doing the right things.

Figure 9-1 compares annual budgeting to strategic planning for the following characteristics:

- Intent
- Time Frame
- Focus
- Level of detail
- Creativity
- Perspective

CONTRASTING ANNUAL BUDGETING WITH STRATEGIC PLANNING

Characteristic	Annual Budgeting & Profit Planning	Strategic Planning
Intent	To control perfor-formance.	To anticipate and plan accordingly.
Time Frame	Short-term. Usually developed annually on a month-by-month basis.	Long-term, most banks usually have a planning horizon from 3 to 7 years.
Focus	Specifies accomplishments that must be achieved by department or organizational unit.	Identifies overall purpose, objectives and goals for both the bank and its SBUs.
Level of Detail	Specific.	Broad.
Creativity	Less creative and more mechanical. More confining in the orientation toward internal operations.	More creative. An opportunity to consider the impact of external factors.
Perspective	Efficiency. To do things right.	Effectiveness. To do the right things.

FIGURE 9-1

How Should the Budget Be Linked to the Strategic Plan?

The bank's annual budget should be consistent with its strategic plan. Although the budget is prepared in considerably greater detail than the strategic plan, it should address the bank's objectives in a manner that is consistent with the strategic plan. Because of the strong tradition of meeting budget, the importance of this internal consistency cannot be overstated. The best laid corporate strategies can be undermined from the onset by a budget that encourages some action different from that called for in the plan. Figure 9-2 illustrates the relative location of the budget in our planning pyramid.

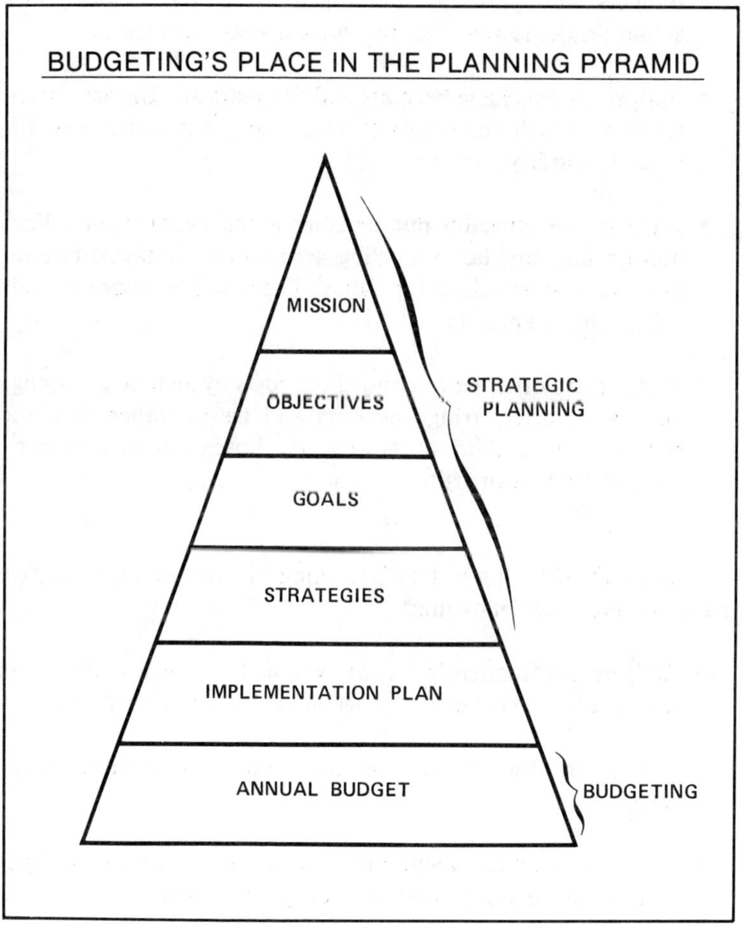

FIGURE 9-2

Management begins with the broadest span of strategic options and then progressively eliminates alternatives until the strategic plan is completed. Once the financial implications of these strategies have been adequately considered, a detailed budget is prepared. Refer to the illustration of Figure 9-3.

The Problem

Simply stated, few banks we have seen do an effective job of linking budgeting to their strategic plan. This is due to several reasons:

- Budgets are generally developed from the prior year's actual results rather than the current year's strategies.
- Budget systems have been around for years and the associated tradition which surrounds their development and use is difficult to modify.
- Budgets are typically put together along departmental lines and do not facilitate reporting across organizational boundaries such as required for SBUs. There will be more on this subject in Chapter 11.
- Budgets are oriented to controlling costs by generic groupings such as salaries, fringe benefits and travel rather than the nature of the activities that generate those costs such as commercial lending or trust accounting.

As a result of failing to link budgeting to strategic planning, we have observed the following:

- Budgets are frequently out of sync with strategies and act as disincentives to the effective accomplishment of bank strategy.
- Meeting the budget is a poor measure of strategic accomplishment.
- A "detailed budget mentality" can, in some cases, be a detriment to achieving a creative strategic environment.
- Tightly controlled "departmental" budgets can counter

LINKAGE OF BUDGETING TO STRATEGY*

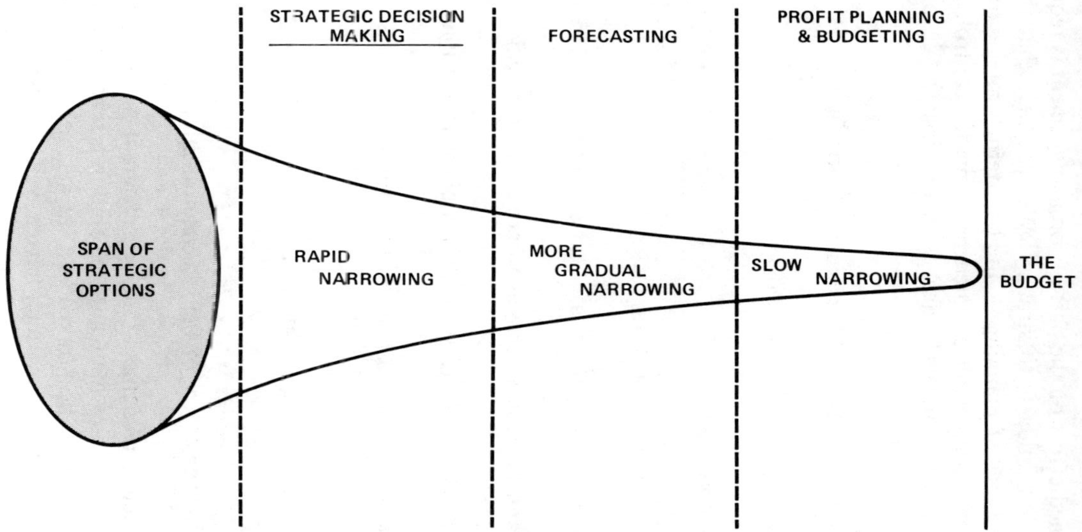

*Adapted from "How to Design a Strategic Planning System" by Lorange and Vancil, *Harvard Business Review*, (September-October) 1976.

FIGURE 9-3

management efforts to get multi-bank disciplines involved on a team basis.

Guidelines for Linking Budgets to Strategy

Determined effort on the part of top management is required to effectively link budgets to strategy. We recognize that the bank needs both types of planning — the long-term strategic tools and the short-term financially oriented performance control. So how can management effectively deal with this issue? We offer the following guidelines:

1. Determine the extent of the interrelationship.
2. Integrate only those items that need to be.
3. Keep things simple.
4. Involve the key operating managers.
5. Avoid extrapolation of last year's results.
6. Recognize and isolate areas where differences exist.
7. Give bank managers as much flexibility as possible.
8. Concentrate only on high priority areas.

Let's consider each guideline in more detail.

1. Determine the extent of the interrelationship.

This guideline recognizes that two different planning processes are involved. The key matter for resolution is what extent the annual budget should be "linked" to the strategic plan. This issue comes up in those banks which have a well established budgeting process that they wish to protect by minimizing the impact of their strategic planning process. To simply translate a budget into some form that corresponds to strategy is difficult, often tedious and frequently raises more questions by creating a third hybrid plan that only the chief planner or cashier understands. *Too tight* a correlation is a crippling disease to strategic management, often referred to as "budget myopia."

2. Integrate only those items that need to be.

More than likely you have heard the cliche: "If it's not broken, don't fix it." Our corollary is: If it is not essential for control or implementation that a certain strategy be tightly linked to a budget figure, then do not link them. Instead, concentrate on those items that:

- Relate directly to key bank values and policies.
- Cover areas where returns and/or risks are material.
- Need details spelled out in order to facilitate communication and commitment to plan.

3. Keep things simple.

No doubt you have heard of the KISS principle (Keep it simple, stupid). In few places does it apply with more force than in linking the annual operating budget to the bank's strategies. Keep the links at the macro level. Look for ways to simplify operating budget data. Avoid unnecessary reconciliations. Remember the principle of materiality and do not get caught up in the mechanics.

4. Involve the key operating managers.

In developing a closer link of strategy to operating budgets, get the bank's key managers involved. Allow them to consider the budget consequences of strategies for which they have responsibility. Let them then develop and finalize the budget with management's review and approval.

5. Avoid extrapolation of last year's results.

Operating budgets should be developed from bank strategies, not from the prior year's financials. Our experience demonstrates that taking last year's numbers and adding 5% or 10% as a point of departure is one of the surest ways we know to undermine the successful implementations of bank strategy.

6. Recognize and isolate areas where differences exist.

Where differences do develop between the budgetary details and the summary financial information contained in the strategic plan, make a reasonable effort to isolate them to an SBU, a location, a product, a department or a set of accounts. This will aid considerably in maintaining the creditability of both the strategic plan and the operating budget while allowing senior bank management to hold the organization accountable for implementing the first year of the business strategy as planned.

7. Give bank managers as much flexibility as possible.

It is vitally important to give key managers as much flexibility and autonomy as possible and still hold true to the overall bank strategy. We have seen too many instances where operating managers had entirely too little flexibility within their operating budget and, as a result, the commitment to implementing strategy soon gave way to the detailed monthly analysis of budget line items.

8. Concentrate only on high priority areas.

The bank CEO and executive management should direct their attention to those key priority areas of strategy that are absolutely critical to the plan's success. In these areas (which could be a particular SBU, a new product line or a particular acquisition), a tighter linkage of short-term budgets to longer-term strategy is particularly important.

To bring the idea of linking the annual budget to the strategic plan into sharper focus, we offer Figure 9-4. It takes a long-range goal and identifies several strategies for each goal. These strategies are then translated into annual goals, explaining what is expected to be accomplished this year. This determines the resources required, if any, and translates them into implications for this year's budget.

Summary

Establishing and streamlining the linkage of business strategy to annual operating budgets is not an easy task. It is complicated by

BOSTON HARBOR COMMUNITY BANK
LINKING THE ANNUAL PLAN
TO THE STRATEGIC PLAN

Strategic Plan		Annual Plan					
		Step 1	Step 2				
Long-Range Goals	Strategies	Annual Goals	Resource Requirements	Budget Implication	Target Begin	Dates End	Responsibility
Hold noninterest expense to 2.75% of average assets for next 5 years	Develop cost & profit centers throughout bank	Identify centers and changes in accounting procedures	Would require new internal project team from several departments	—	3/15	5/31	Robert Johnson
	Develop reporting systems to monitor productivity	Reexamine allocation methods employed in the banks	Could be done by existing cost accounting personnel	—			
	Consider use of part-time staff			-$20,000			New Personnel Director
Implement asset liability management system to monitor net interest spread at 4.25% of average assets	Redefine organization responsibilities	Develop new ALCO charter	Attend BAI or other seminar/training	+ $5,000	1/20	2/28	Art Jones
	Develop new computer model	Research available software	Involve outside consultant if necessary	+ $8,000	4/1	6/1	Mary Cathy

FIGURE 9-4

the fact that many banks evolved to a point of developing strategic plans from the preparation of detail budgets and forecasts. And, although budgets are developed with a much narrower focus and more detail, they are critical to successfully managing the implementation of strategy.

The key point to remember is that strategy must drive budgets, not vice versa. The two planning processes cannot co-exist long without attention being given to their ultimate integration. Remember not to let the mechanics of budget preparation narrow the spectrum of the bank's strategic alternatives or interfere with the planning climate that is essential to develop and implement effective strategy.

10 STRATEGY TRANSLATION AND MOTIVATION

"There is nothing more frightful than ignorance in action."
... Goethe

In the last several chapters we have developed the strategic planning process to address successive levels of detail. We have gone from very broad mission statements covering many years to detailed annual plans that direct the bank's short-term efforts. The focus has been on the plan itself and on the people who organized and implemented it. What we have not yet considered in detail is how to personalize the plan for those individuals whose performance will determine whether or not the plan is accomplished. Thus, the purpose of this chapter is to discuss how to:

- Translate bank strategies into individual's performance objectives.
- Communicate strategies to key operating personnel.
- Motivate personnel to channel their efforts toward strategy accomplishment.

Importance of Strategy Translation and Motivation

In our associations with various banks over the last several years, we have repeatedly encountered senior executives who are having considerable difficulty getting everyone moving in the same direction and focusing on accomplishing the same objectives. Regardless of how "great" the strategic plan is, if employees either do not know how bank objectives translate into what's expected of them or are not motivated to accomplish them, then very little of the plan will be successful.

For example, the strategic plan may call for more fee income, but observations reveal very little cross-selling of bank services. Tellers are not asking their customers about their plans for opening an IRA. Loan officers are failing to encourage borrowers to purchase credit life insurance policies or consider other bank services like brokerage, escrow and cash management. In essence, the plan calls for, and the CEO wants, more fee income, but how does this get instilled in the operating personnel? The answer to that question is the subject of this chapter.

We believe management's ability to successfully execute strategy has a direct relationship on how well they translate strategy into key performance objectives and how effectively they are in motivating key employees. The benefits of effective translation and motivation include:

- Better internal communication.
- Enhanced ability to achieve annual goals.
- Faster implementation of strategy.
- Improved monitoring of performance.

Nature of Strategy Motivation

To facilitate strategy implementation by the organization, senior management must first recognize the tremendous importance and value of individual efforts within the bank. Key operating managers and employees should have that sense of "strategic ownership" that results in the type of collective focus and personal energy necessary to implement strategy successfully.

Motivation begins with the individual knowing what's expected of him. Our experience indicates that many key bank employees do not know management's expectations. Our basic formula for motivation is not unique:

- Identify the contributions an individual can make.
- Challenge the individual.
- Recognize his achievement.

We believe that the successful translation of strategy and the motivation of key individuals to carry it is a fundamental part of strategic management. Implemented properly, it can do much to insure the successful execution of strategy.

Figure 10-1 illustrates the goal of strategy translation and motivation — the achievement of goal congruence between the bank as an entity and the key managers as individuals.

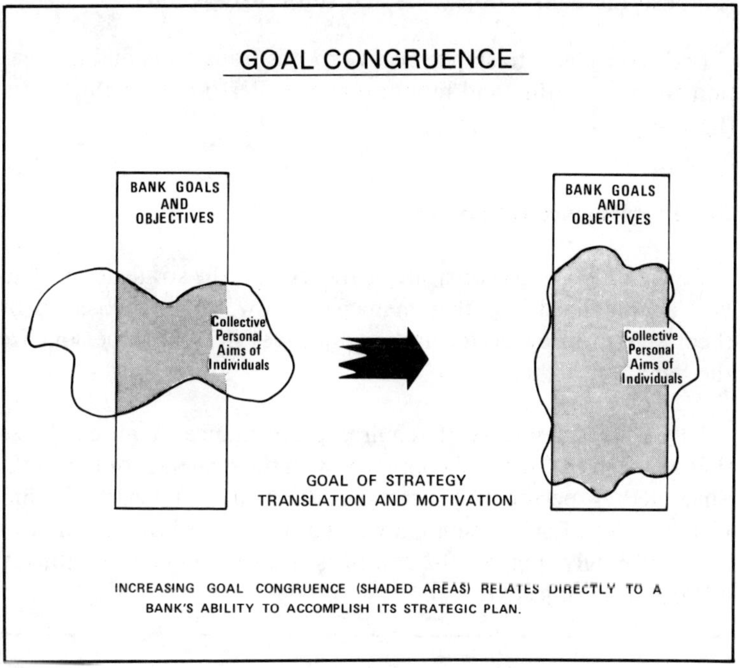

FIGURE 10-1

Management's job is to translate the strategies in a manner that motivates individuals to alter their personal goals to align them more closely with the bank's. This is accomplished by:

- Identifying the contributions an individual can make.
- Communicating what is expected from him.
- Challenging the individual.
- Recognizing his achievement.
- Rewarding him.

We have observed how important proper translation, communication and motivation are to successful execution of strategy. Without the knowledge of what is expected of them, key employees may direct their efforts to tasks that are either unrelated to the critical tasks or even contradictory to them. Unless employees are instilled with that sense of strategic ownership of the bank's goals, the CEO will continue to be frustrated in his attempts to accomplish the bank's objectives and fulfill its mission.

Let's consider a fresh perspective to this translation and motivation issue — setting and monitoring Key Performance Objectives (KPOs).

Key Performance Objectives

To create this sense of strategic ownership, the strategies need to be "personalized" so that managers know what is expected of them. We use Key Performance Objectives (KPOs) to personalize the bank's strategies.

KPOs are statements of required performance by an employee that are derived from and consistent with the strategies of the bank. Since KPOs personalize strategies, they aid immensely in implementation. Each person knows what is expected of him and can act accordingly. Figure 10-2 contrasts strategic objectives with key performance objectives.

STRATEGIC VS. KEY PERFORMANCE OBJECTIVES

Strategic Objective	Key Performance Objective
Generalized	Personalized
Defines the overall course of action for the bank as a whole or a significant operating group	Answers the question as to what a specific individual's responsibility is in strategy implementation
Longer-term planning horizon (typically more than one year).	Short-term planning horizon (Typically one year).
Less detail	More detail

FIGURE 10-2

Characteristics of key performance objectives include:

- Direct relationship to strategy
- Pertain only to critical operating managers
- Accepted by management
- Internally consistent
- Timely
- Measurable
- Simple and concise

The establishment of key performance objectives provides a means to clearly convey the strategies to be achieved and a mechanism for management to monitor progress. The quantity of information generated by a KPO system is intentionally lean, since it addresses only the most critical strategic success factors of the bank. It provides a small amount of highly structured information to senior management on a consistent basis and lessens the potential for data deluge.

The unit of measure for a KPO is called a Key Performance Indicator (KPI). Key performance indicators are objective and subjective factors that *measure* the accomplishment of key performance objectives. The key performance indicator answers the question: How do I know that I am meeting the key performance objective?

To better illustrate the concept of key performance objectives and key performance indicators, consider the example in Figure 10-3.

We believe, that to the extent that a simplified *network* of KPOs and KPIs can be established, the greater are the chances of successfully implementing the strategic plan. We like this technique because we have seen it work where most traditional approaches break down.

Problems with Traditional Approaches

Management By Objectives (MBO) — MBO programs usually

ILLUSTRATION OF KEY PERFORMANCE OBJECTIVES

TRANSLATION & MOTIVATION HIERARCHY	DEFINITION	EXAMPLE
Strategic Success Factors ↓	Success Factors which are critical to attainment of strategic ends. Those factors of performance that must receive consistent and continuous management attention to successfully execute the strategies of the bank.	The ability of the bank to obtain adequate capital to finance future growth.
Key Performance Objectives ↓	Statements of required performance for critical managers consistent with the bank's strategic objectives. Their accomplishment is necessary to ensure successful strategy implementation.	To improve the bank's capital position, the executive vice president is responsible for improving the profitability of branch operation by $450,000 over the next 12 months.
Key Performance Indicators	Measures at specific intervals of time which track key individual's progress against specific short-term goals.	• Cost per branch transaction. • Total branch payroll cost. • Increases in branch service charge income.

FIGURE 10-3

establish key performance measures, but do so on the basis of negotiation with the employee rather than focusing on bank strategy. MBO programs typically include all employees above a certain level, rather than only those critical to strategy implementation. In addition, performance information is not communicated at frequent enough intervals. Usually, the program is not automated, does not contain "what-if" capabilities and lacks the comprehensive data base needed by management to probe reasons for performance variances. Although MBO may include some key performance information, it lacks the depth and focus of a KPO system.

Key Factor Reporting — Key factor reporting for senior management is used by many banks. However, most key factor information systems are not designed to be directly related to bank strategy. Since they do not distinguish between strategic and operating information, they overload executives with too many operating statistics. Typically, they sacrifice strategic information for operating data.

Responsibility Reporting — Responsibility reporting is a technique which has been available for many years. Although its objectives are similar to a KPO system, it typically focuses on only one strategic success factor — the control of costs. In addition, a responsibility reporting system uses historical data which does not necessarily measure critical aspects of bank strategy. Also, in the typical level by level roll-up of data, key information is often obscured by the summarization process.

How to Implement an Effective KPO System

The process for implementing an effective system of key performance objectives is illustrated in Figure 10-4 and discussed in this section.

Step 1: Select the Strategic Success Factors — You should recall from Chapter 3, Strategic Success Factors (SSFs) are that limited number of factors which are critical to the attainment of bank strategy. They are those areas of performance selected by senior management which must receive careful, continuous, consistent and conspicuous management attention to successfully execute the strategies. Information regarding SSFs may not be available as a

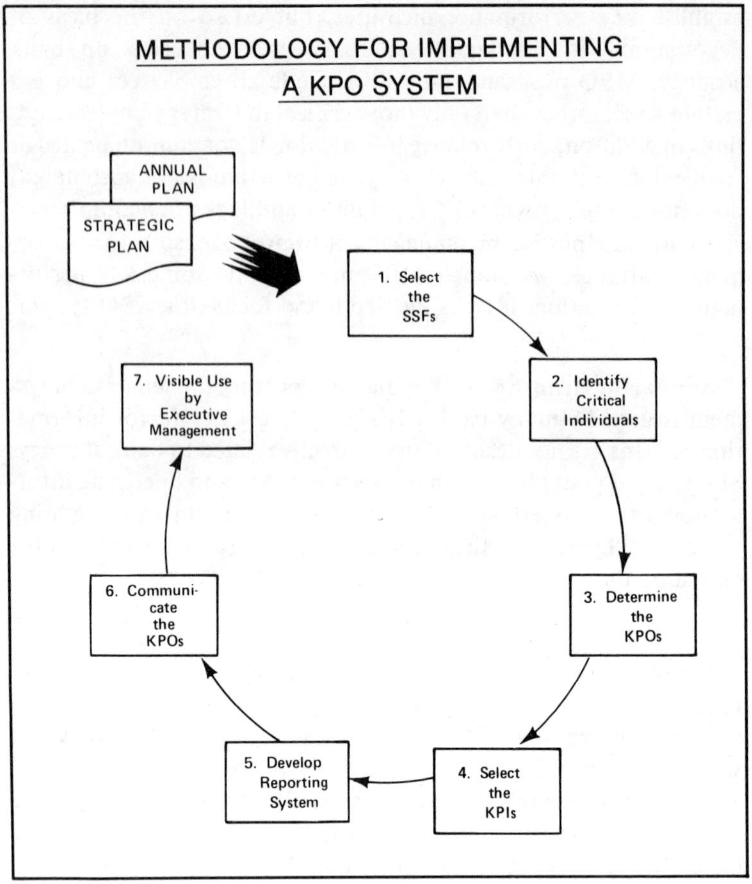

FIGURE 10-4

by-product of bank transaction systems. They will likely require external data, which may be challenging to quantify.

Step 2: Identify Critical Individuals — Managers whose performance is critical to attainment of the SSFs must be identified. These key personnel form the nucleus of a cadre of managers whose performance will determine the future of the bank. If the key managers are otherwise incapable of achieving the designated SSFs, senior management should consider the appropriateness of changing the current organization.

Step 3: Determine the Key Performance Objectives — Key performance objectives should stimulate individuals to achieve SSFs and can provide frequent visibility of their performance. They must be explicit to motivate managers and to convince them that their actions influence the strategic success of the bank.

Step 4: Select the Key Performance Indicators — KPIs are used to measure the short-term performance of the individuals whose performance is critical to strategy accomplishment. They should be encompassing and reasonably complete, otherwise there may be a misunderstanding of the effort necessary to accomplish the KPOs.

Step 5: Develop a Reporting System — The development of a reporting system begins with a plan. First, determine the availability of information on the strategic success factors and other key performance information. If this information is not available from existing bank systems, then it must be developed through additional systems work. Such work might include the development of the functional and technical requirements of the reporting system and the specification of the hardware and software environment.

The type of delivery system developed will depend, of course, on the quantity and type of information needed, and on management's style and philosophy. For example, top management may want to explore underlying causes of an eroding capital base. Or senior bank executives may desire to ask "what-if" questions and to receive responses quickly in a graphic format.

Step 6: Communicate the KPOs — The method of initially communicating the final set of key performance objectives and indicators to "the critical individuals" is very important. Before actually implementing the new reporting system, meetings should be held with senior management and the critical individuals to discuss the performance indicators. Four basic points should be emphasized at these meetings:

- The bank's future depends on successfully implementing its strategies.
- The key performance objectives and indicators are based on these strategies.
- Performance indicators will be monitored by senior management.
- Recognition, promotion and financial remuneration will be affected by individual and group performance.

Step 7: Visible Use by Executive Management — For a KPO system to be successful, it must be conspicuously used by the bank's senior executives. Management can show they value the information by using it to evaluate the performance of their subordinates.

Relationship to Existing Bank Systems

In developing a KPO system, you may find that it is out of sync with other bank systems. It could be in conflict with:

- Incentive methods
- Personnel systems (including MBO's)
- Executive bonus programs
- Departmental cost reporting

Bank management should recognize that this is likely to occur and take the necessary steps over a reasonable period of time to bring other systems in line with the key performance objective system.

Summary

In summary, we believe management's ability to successfully execute strategies depends on how well they have translated them into key performance objectives and how effectively they motivate key employees.

11 STRATEGIC INFORMATION SYSTEMS

"For whatever deserves to exist deserves also to be known, for knowledge is the image of existence."

... Francis Bacon

Information is increasingly being recognized as not simply an important business resource, but a critical one. This is particularly true for bankers where meaningful economic data, competitive intelligence, and timely reporting oriented toward management action can make the difference between financial success or failure.

What would information similar to the following be worth to your bank?

- Knowing that one of your competitors is going to offer real estate loans two full percentage points lower than the current market rate.
- Knowing probable government actions regarding international trade restrictions or exchange controls in a market area of your bank.
- Knowing that a competitor plans to open an ATM in the small shopping center dominated by one of your branches.
- Knowing that major tax legislation that will significantly enhance desirability of certain bank services/products will soon be proposed.

Can you realistically even give such information a value? Probably not. Intrinsically, however, the value of information depends upon its being timely, reliable, and focused on some relevant business decision.

Much has been written and said about the information age, the impact of microcomputers on business, and the explosion of high technology into banking. This we will not repeat. We will, however, consider the definition of strategic information systems and its role in the formulation and execution of bank strategy.

What Is a Strategic Information System?

The basis for formulating and executing effective strategy is information. One of the best means for supporting and enhancing the strategic management process is the use of strategic information systems. In this chapter, we are taking a broad "generic" view of the word "system" to include a well organized approach to data collection and analysis. Such a system may deal with the external economic environment, direct competitive situations, and/or the viability of new products and services. It could also take various forms from a totally manual system to one that is highly automated.

Regardless of the form, a strategic information system should have these features:

- Timely information.

  The need for timely data in strategic systems almost invariably involves a sacrifice of accuracy. Strategic information systems recognize the "time value" of information.

- Quick accessibility.

  Information delivery and accessibility is critical for management in order to arrange relevant information in a manner that is truly supportive to key decisions being made.

- Merging of internal and external data.

  Integrating internal and external data allows management to evaluate operating results in light of competitors' performance, determine changes in market share, and consider the financial implication of economic events.

- Security.

  Security involves controlling access to critical bank records, files and reports. It should be apparent that security surrounding strategic information is a high priority that deserves management attention.

• Adaptable to changing needs.

Strategic systems should be flexible enough to change as the strategic factors themselves change. New information may cause the strategic plans to be modified or updated. Strategic information systems must be able to accommodate these changes and to report them in a manner that facilitates management consideration.

Strategic vs. Traditional Bank Systems

Most bank systems are large transaction processors, designed to handle large volumes of data and to assist in controlling day to day operations. Many are oriented toward daily balancing and cost control. A few others consider revenue enhancements, but most have clerical efficiency in mind. These traditional systems have included demand deposit accounting, installment loan processing, portfolio management, time certificates of deposit, etc.

Contrast this, if you will, to strategic information systems whose major purpose is to enhance management effectiveness and productivity. These systems are planning-oriented, decision driven, used actively by executives, and incorporate external as well as internal data.

Conventional systems are developed by a bottom-up approach, guessing what bank management wants to see. Strategic systems, however, are driven down from the top. Figure 11-1 summarizes these differences in tabular form.

The Delivery Characteristics of Strategic Systems

Much has been written recently about the changes occurring in the bank's delivery systems to its market. ATMs, electronic home banking and EFTS have significantly altered the more traditional branch delivery system. There is a close analogy here to the changes that are taking place internally in the bank's own systems and data processing capabilities.

The results-oriented demands of management have led to a greater emphasis on "decision support systems." We define such a system as a set of functions or applications which augment a manager's planning and decision making process. "End-user com-

CONVENTIONAL VS. STRATEGIC SYSTEMS

Conventional Data Processing System	Strategic Information System
• Passive use	• Active use
• Clerical activities	• Line, management and staff activities
• Oriented toward mechanical efficiency	• Oriented toward overall effectiveness
• Focus on the past	• Focus on the present and future
• Emphasis on consistency	• Emphasis on flexibility
• Internal data exclusively	• Includes external data
• Static in nature	• Dynamic in nature

FIGURE 11-1

puting," once considered a fantasy, is now a reality with advent of microcomputers, electronic spreadsheets and sophisticated graphic presentations of information.

Even the way strategic systems are developed is changing. No longer are all such systems turned over to the centralized computer department for long-term development efforts. More often such systems are being developed, installed and used under a "prototype" approach. Under this method of development, certain strategic systems can be brought up quickly, then enhanced and improved as senior bank management works with it and the system gains credibility.

Bank Examples of Strategic Information Systems

There are a number of strategic information systems for banks. This section will briefly present a few such examples:

- Image Information System

- Asset/Liability Management
- Modeling and Forecasting
- Competitive Intelligence System
- Prospect Information System

Image Information System

The competitive nature of the financial services market has forced banks to find out how they are viewed by their customers and the community. In contrast to heavy quantitative, analytical information systems, gathering data on image is a much "softer" area.

Customer surveys is a well-accepted technique used to determine bank image. These surveys ask questions about why customers selected your bank. They may ask one to rate the friendliness of the tellers, convenience of facilities, or speed of service. In addition, surveys often ask if one has an auto or home improvement loan, any accounts at other banks, etc.

Traditionally, there has been an all-out effort to collect such customer information every few years. What we see emerging is a need for *more frequent* collection of information about customers' perception of the bank. This allows the bank to determine *changes* or shifts in attitudes and perceptions that is needed to help formulate bank strategy.

In addition, we see a need for more focused efforts in determining the required information. Too often the collected customer and image data are interesting, but do not relate to bank strategy. If your bank's mission at the bank is to be a leader in innovating new products, for example, customer surveys should be used to gather data on the extent of acceptance of those new products and the *reasons* behind the acceptance or rejection.

We have not seen traditional systems in the classic sense be developed that genuinely monitor image. We believe they will become more widespread as banks strive to differentiate themselves from their competitors.

Asset/Liability Management System

Asset and liability management has emerged in recent years as an important strategic tool for planning and improving bank profits. Such a system involves:

- A methodical decomposition and analysis of the bank's balance sheet structure on a continuous basis.

- Improved understanding of the key characteristics of a bank's sources and uses of funds, liquidity, quality, rate-sensitivity and margins.

- The formation and organization of a competent asset/liability management team.

Well designed systems facilitate the following:

- The review of changes in economic conditions and interest rate projections.

- Comparison and analysis of actual to targeted net interest margin and rate sensitivity.

- Forecasts of future account balances, net interest margin, inflation rates, growth trends, changes in product mix and rate sensitivity.

- Development of management recommendations regarding Fed Funds position, tax, adequacy of loan loss reserve, dividends, liquidity and capital adequacy.

- Review of the bank's investment portfolio and the formulation of investment strategy.

Figure 11-2 highlights some of the major reports which should be the output of an effective asset/liability management system.

We hope by now most bankers have some form of an asset/liability management system since they are at the core of many critical decisions. The key is how well it really works. Does it measure the micro as well as the macro gaps? Does it genuinely facilitate formulating strategies that might involve hedging or

MAJOR ASSET/LIABILITY MANAGEMENT REPORTS	
Report	Function/Comments
Economic Analysis	Summarize the key interest rate projection for the near term. Projections should be supported by outside research and revised at least monthly.
Rate Sensitivity Analysis	Indicates the percentage of sources and use of funds that are rate sensitive for selected time periods (such as 90, 180, 270, 360 days). This report should facilitate the better matching of assets and liabilities for the intermediate and longer term. It should also be set up with specific targets to facilitate the monitoring of bank progres.
Interest Rate Risk Exposure	Notes how much the bank's interest would increase or decrease if interest rates were to change one percent.
Run-Off Schedules	Shows asset or liability by fixed and variable rates and its maturity period.
Net Interest Margin Analysis	Indicates why net interest margin has increased or decreased from the prior period to aid in future planning. Should show both current month and year to date results to facilitate analysis of rate and volume change.

FIGURE 11-2

sophisticated interest rate swaps? If not, the opportunities exist to make a good planning and analysis tool a truly strategic system.

Modeling and Forecasting

Modeling enables management to evaluate the consequences of policy and action alternatives. In the broadest sense it includes assimilation of economic data and incorporates it into bank planning and decision making.

Models are both a system and a technique. A model may have an identity of its own or be a tool contained within system. For example, most meaningful asset/liability systems offer bank executives some "what if" or modeling capability.

The most successful models we have observed are quite deterministic in nature. That is, they are designed to answer "if/then" questions. Other modeling techniques, such as optimization and simulation approaches, are most effective in isolated situations which involve limited and specific, well-known relationships. More recently we have seen organizations approach modeling through an organized network of simple models interconnected such that each could stand alone or be executed collectively.

Modeling is useful in assisting management to isolate variables and assess their impact upon bank operations. Models offer a low risk method of analyzing alternatives and are particularly useful in assisting management avoid mistakes.

Competitive Intelligence Systems

In the chapter on environmental scanning, we discussed the need for competitor profiles. They provide you with the information necessary to identify your most significant competitors, determine their strengths and weaknesses and assess their strategic position within your market. Preparing these profiles requires information that should be gathered through a competitive intelligence system.

A competitive intelligence system is an organized on-going effort focused on collecting information about each competitor (existing and potential). This information is collected in trickles over time, and when put together yields a comprehensive picture of your competitor. Since Chapters 3 and 4 included specific examples of competitive profiles and their role in developing strategy, this discussion focuses on the data collection dimensions of a competitive intelligence system.

Collecting *published* data is the most straightforward. The sources of competitive data include newspapers, banking journals, financial reports, newsletters and competitor mailings (someone in your bank should be on the mailing list of each of your competitors). These and other sources are identified in the Appendix. Responsibility for reviewing the published sources and collecting the relevant information should be clearly identified. This effort should be coordinated through the planning officer.

Collecting *field* data involves more ingenuity and certainly more subtlety. Sources of field data include such things as speeches by your competitors' management, discussions at professional meetings, and your own employees. One approach is to have someone from your bank periodically visit your competitors' lobbies and observe what is going on there. How busy are their tellers? How long are their lines? Another approach is to have your loan officer submit any information about your competitors that they have received from their current and prospective customers.

For a competitor intelligence system to be effective, both the published and field data must be assembled at a centralized collection point. This may be as simple as a file folder for each competitor. Responsibility for coordinating a competitor intelligence system is typically given to the planning officer. In addition, someone other than the planning officer should periodically take a major competitor's file, review it, and make a presentation to other executives of the bank about the changes in the competitor's posture. For a major competitor this may take place as often as once a quarter or twice a year. The most comprehensive systems we have observed included the presentation of one or more sophisticated competitive profiles at each planning meeting. This forces the presenter to search for gaps in the competitor's profile and initiate collection efforts. Figure 11-3 illustrates the major characteristics of a competitive intelligence system.

Prospect Information System

The purpose of a prospect information system is to target major potential clients. It involves collecting external data for sorting out potential clients and subsequently gathering more information on how target prospects should be approached. Why is a particular prospect strategically important to you? Would it mean penetration into a new market? How profitable an account would it be? Are their board members influential with other companies included on each loan executive's call sheet? These are questions which should be addressed by this system.

In order to promote your bank, you must demonstrate you understand a prospect's business. How can you demonstrate this understanding in a manner that will move a prospect to consider your bank? What are his current banking arrangements? What services can you offer and at what cost? When should they be approached and by whom?

POTENTIAL CHARACTERISTICS OF A COMPETITIVE INTELLIGENCE SYSTEM*

- Centralized files coordinated by the planning officer.
- Competitor profiles that focus on what "drives" the competitor.
  - Are they satisfied with the current position?
  - What moves will they likely make?
  - Where is the competitor vulnerable?
  - What will provoke the greatest and most effective retaliation by the competitor?
- Data collection techniques.
  - Clipping services for information about competitors.
  - Interviewing individuals who come into contact with competitors.
  - Personal observations of competitors' operations.
- Data ranked by reliability of the source.
- Periodic situation reports on competitors by selected management.
- Examination of competitor profiles by selected management.

*Adapted from: **Competitive Strategy** by Michael E. Porter, 1980, The Free Press.

FIGURE 11-3

A prospect information system is the natural result of mounting competition among financial service organizations for key accounts. At present it is, more often than not, a manual system.

Technical Considerations

The various strategic information systems that we have discussed in this chapter lend themselves in varying degrees to automation. As with any automation effort, there are certain technical considerations. For strategic information systems, there are two technical dimensions we wish to discuss:

- Data base management.
- End user computing.

Effective **Data Base Management** involves the organization and accessibility of data so that it is understood by the user. Today this dimension is facilitated by numerous software products using high-level languages with powerful data manipulation, retrieval and presentation techniques. The major challenges facing the architect of such computer systems is developing an easy to comprehend data organization, categorizing external and internal sources of data as well as monitoring the time dimension of various items of information. These challenges can quickly become quite complex technically.

Decisions are required regarding the level of detail data that must be stored and how to maintain a system that is essentially evolutionary in its development and use. Flexibility typically becomes a dominant requirement as does rapid access to data and fast, management-oriented reporting.

End User Computing is now a reality with the assistance from personal and micro computers. Computer software has become more user firendly, highly interactive, more flexible, and certainly a great deal more powerful. Report writers, electronic spread sheets and graphic oriented presentations have facilitated the value of computerized tools immensely.

There have been other developments and trends emerging in the area of office automation that may deserve banker attention.

- The establishment of "information centers" within an organization to facilitate the assimilation and analysis of internal and external data.
- The integration of strategic planning and information processing into a closer working partnership.
- The designation of a "chief information officer" to coordinate "information delivery systems" and the use of information in executive decisions.

Banks will need to pay more attention in the future to the trends in office automation. As these systems become commonplace for the business executive, it is forecasted that these techniques will shrink the need for middle management as executives rely more and more upon the computer for information. Various decision support and strategic systems will enhance executive effectiveness by providing immediate feedback about alternatives under consideration.

Problems Encountered with Strategic Information Systems

There is one fundamental problem which is typically encountered with the installation of strategic information systems — the emergence of different sets of data. This problem can be significant, particularly where the traditional systems are basically archaic and unresponsive to management's needs. By way of illustration, consider these examples of the differences and disparities caused by different sets of data.

- Financial data used to calculate market share by product line is different from current financial statements. Does the bank use internal data that has the same time lag as external competitive data? How are reserves and non-accruals considered in examining market shares of the loan portfolio?

- The runoff schedules used in a bank's asset/liability management model are different from balances carried in the bank's various loan systems. Are these differences due to cutoff problems? Is it the nature of summarizations? How are participations are accounted for? Are there differences in pricing schemes and methods of determining effective yield?

The consequences of multiple data sets could be indecision, time wasted on validating the numbers to get at the true facts, negative second-guessing, and the development of a lack of confidence in management decision making.

The answer to avoiding such a situation is to *effectively integrate* your bank's strategic information systems with its traditional accounting and control applications. Most banks we know are discovering that accomplishing this legitimate objective is quite difficult for several reasons:

- Cutoff problems are encountered that contributed significantly to differences between the accurate historical focus of accounting data and the real-time estimates needed for some strategic systems.

- Traditional bank systems have a profit center, cost center or department orientation and not the SBU perspective that is needed. Refer to Figure 11-4.
- Their linkage between the strategic plan and the bank's operating plans is minimum.

Overcoming Integration Problems

There are no easy solutions to overcoming the integration difficulties associated with strategic information systems. However, we offer this advice for those who relate to the situation:

- Do not waste several years trying to design the "ultimate MIS" that operates from a single data set.
- Adopt a state of mind that addresses any differences as follows:
  - — If things can be easily integrated, do it.
  - — If data cannot be easily integrated, assess the risks involved.
  - — Do whatever you can to minimize these risks.
- Recognize the "time value of information" just as you recognize the time value of money.

Guidelines for Implementing Strategic Information Systems

It is not our intent to describe a systems development methodology for constructing strategic information systems. Much has been written about developing systems successfully and there is no need to repeat it. There are, however, a few guidelines and items to be remembered which are worth noting:

1. Remember a system should be defined broadly as a "coordination of actions," and not merely considered as a computer program.

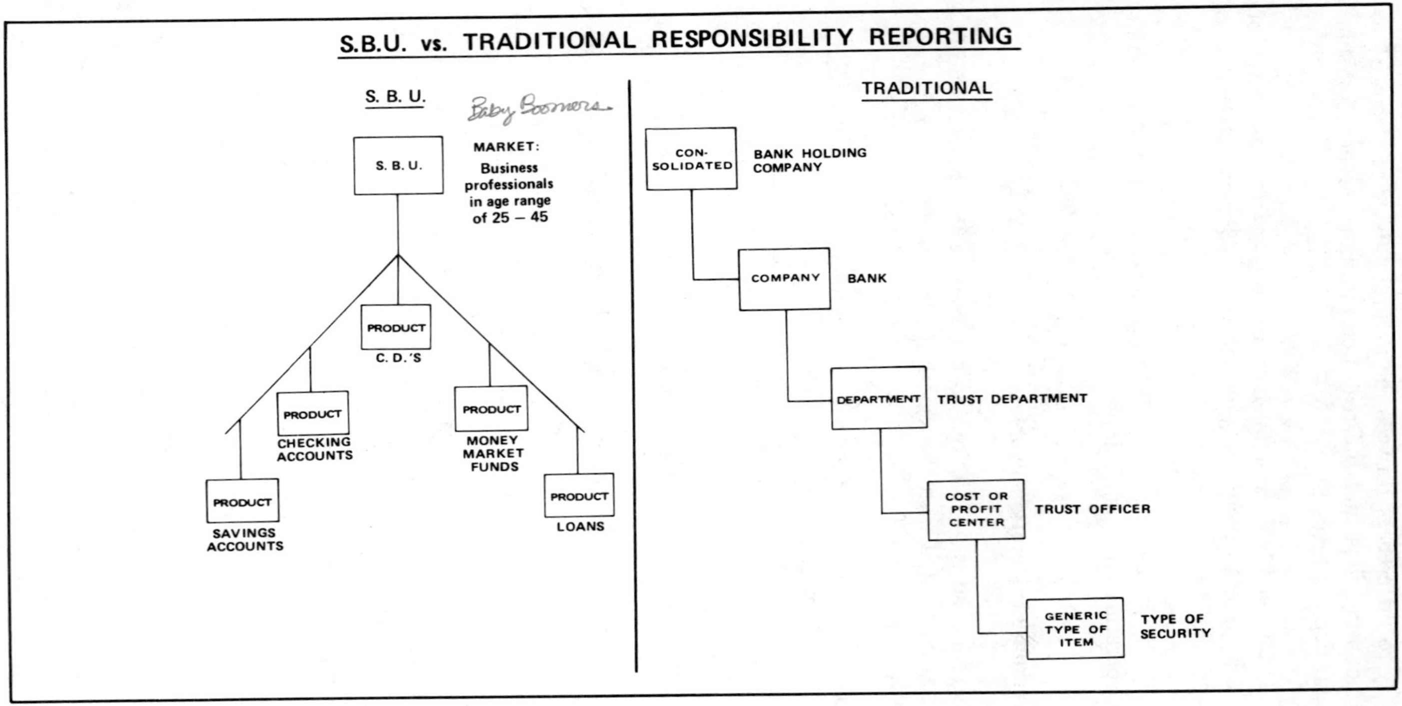
S.B.U. vs. TRADITIONAL RESPONSIBILITY REPORTING
S. B. U.
S. B. U.
MARKET: Business professionals in age range of 25 – 45
PRODUCT
SAVINGS ACCOUNTS
PRODUCT
CHECKING ACCOUNTS
PRODUCT
C. D.'S
PRODUCT
MONEY MARKET FUNDS
PRODUCT
LOANS
TRADITIONAL
CON-SOLIDATED
BANK HOLDING COMPANY
COMPANY
BANK
DEPARTMENT
TRUST DEPARTMENT
COST OR PROFIT CENTER
TRUST OFFICER
GENERIC TYPE OF ITEM
TYPE OF SECURITY

FIGURE 11-4

2. Push management needs down from the top.

3. Do not confuse operating data and statistics with strategic information.

4. Initiate a technical planning capability for testing business assumptions.

5. Ensure that your executives are comfortable with personal computers.

6. Emphasize meaningful information displays.

7. Consider establishing a focal point for strategic information.

8. Focus on the delivery system (decision support, data base management, end user computing, etc.).

9. Concentrate on the present and the future.

10. Pay attention to your strategic success factors (SSF's)!

11. Emphasize value added efforts.

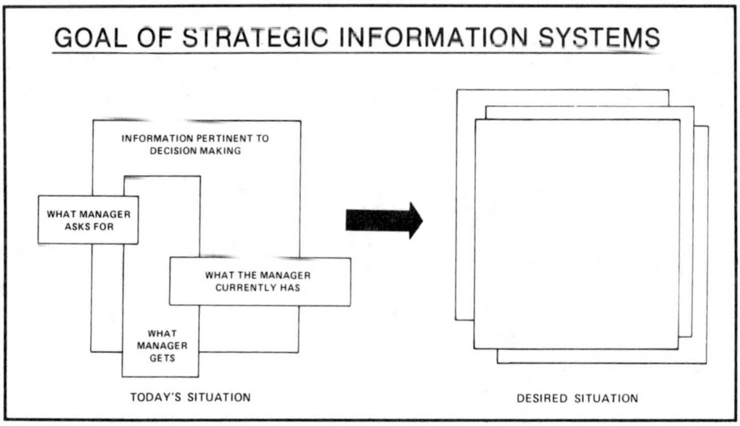

FIGURE 11-5

The Future for Strategic Information Systems

The exciting thing about strategic information systems is their excellent future. With technological advances constantly occurring, the tools you as management need to access information are becoming more accessible all the time.

Aside from technology, management is recognizing the "time value of information" and putting demands on the development of strategic systems because of their importance in securing competitive advantage. External data is also given added emphasis. The orientation is finally reversing — systems are being forced into the framework of management decision making, rather than management decisions being framed by what the system allows.

In summary, the future looks bright. It is up to you to take advantage of it.

STRATEGIC THINKING

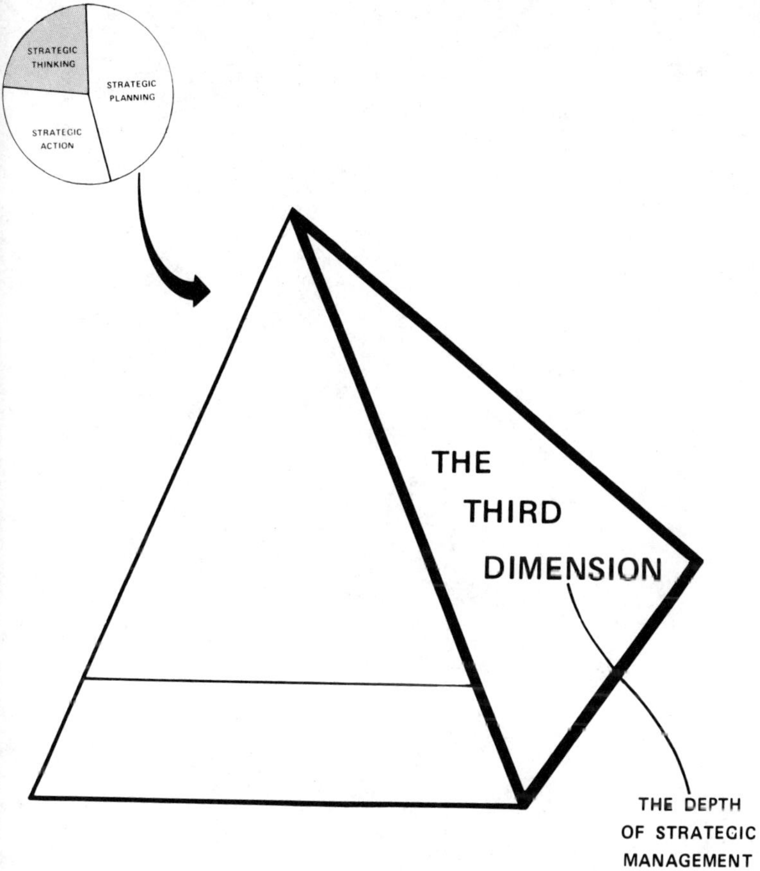

CHAPTERS 12-14

12 THE USE OF STRATEGIC THINKING

"Man's mind, stretched to a new idea, never goes back to its original dimension."

... *Oliver Wendell Holmes*

To this point, the presentation has concentrated on the details of how to develop and implement a strategic plan. Now we shift gears to a conceptual discussion about STRATEGIC THINKING, that elusive ingredient that changes the nature of your strategic plan from a static document to a dynamic management tool.

What Is Strategic Thinking?

The best way to understand what we mean by strategic thinking is to first understand what it is not. Strategic thinking is not a:

- Document.
- One time annual effort.
- Mere articulation of current thinking.
- First step of getting a budget.

Strategic thinking does not manifest itself in any tangible product, but can be observed through the quality and substance of the products of the strategic planning process. Without strategic thinking the planning process is lifeless.

We define *strategic thinking* as the ability to direct the mind to see its surroundings from multiple perspectives. Strategic thinkers can look at the same data or situation as others but see alternative and innovative ways of explaining or solving it. Their thinking is not bounded by tradition such that they can only see things in the light of how it was done in the past. Instead, they go beyond and provide the creative insights that are the essential ingredients to strategic management.

Within the banking industry especially, the boundaries around the decision alternatives are constricted by rigid, traditional beliefs. Many bankers are reluctant to challenge certain assumptions and methods of doing business. They continue to make decisions based on what has worked in the past. Hence, fresh insights and innovations from middle and lower managers are rare. Strategic thinking, on the other hand, requires unlearning many of the rules that governed past actions. It can be done. Psychologists find that people who think they are creative, are creative but those that believe they are not creative are not. It is a self-fulfilling prophecy. A strategic thinker believes he has insights into problems that others do not have and his fresh ideas will lead somewhere. Senior management must create an environment where each employee believes he can creatively contribute to the future of the bank.

Creating the Proper Climate

To get everyone to start thinking strategically the CEO must establish a climate that encourages and rewards such behavior. Initial steps would include:

- Involving all employees in the planning process.
- Soliciting employees' options on an informal basis.
- Encouraging participation in professional organizations.
- Conducting meetings to discuss such things as competition, customers, regulations and services.

Beyond these initial steps, a strategic thinking climate also requires that you set aside a special time, without interruptions, for employees to think about their business and ways to improve it. These sessions may be as formal as thinktanks and retreats or as informal as backroom brainstorming sessions. By their nature, these sessions usually provide an opportunity for cross stimulation of ideas with all the resulting synergistic effects. They produce the kind of thinking that generally does not occur if an employee were working alone.

To be effective, some ground rules should be established. First, participants should suspend judgments on all ideas until late in the session. A foolish, wild idea left on the table long enough may stimulate someone else to come up with a useful idea. Second, everyone enters the meeting on equal footing. Dominance by senior managers or peer group leaders inhibits participation by others. Third, there should be no repercussions for being wrong. We often see too much importance attached to being right all of the time. As a result, we find the fear of being wrong is the biggest impediment to expressing new ideas. We will discuss more on this in Chapter 13.

Some techniques proven to be effective in stimulating strategic thinking include:

- Problem Restatement - restating the problem in a variety of ways may lead to insights into the nature of the problem that were not obvious originally.

- Multiple Solutions - instead of searching for what seems to be one right answer, employees should look for a second, third, and fourth right answer.

- What If Questions - this allows you to suspend the rules of the game, adjust some assumptions and establish a germinal frame of mind. The bank can even have a "What if..." question already on the agenda. For example, what if the cost of money doubled in the next six months? The more contrary-to-fact the "what if" question is, the more provocative and stimulating is the discussion.

Even with the aid of several techniques, the proper planning culture does not just happen. It must be created, nurtured, and supported by the CEO.

Post-Plan Strategic Thinking

Often those involved in strategic planning consider strategic thinking completed when the annual planning process is complete. Our experience shows that nothing could be further from the truth. We have found that a finished plan merely signals the beginning of a new round of strategic thinking, with the first item on the agenda being to challenge the current plan.

- What assumptions were correct or incorrect?

- What was successful or unsuccessful about the plan?

This kind of examination stimulates new insights on how the bank relates to its environment. It generates alternatives for each problem area. These in turn are evaluated and become inputs to the next planning go-round.

As a continuing effort, employees should be constantly monitoring events in both the internal and external environments. This helps the employee not only obtain knowledge of his own bank, but also to develop insights into the relationship between the bank and its environment. He then can apply these insights not only to next year's plan but also to daily decision making.

Benefits of Strategic Thinking

Strategic thinking is the depth of the planning pyramid. It transforms an unstable two-dimensional triangle into a stable, upright pyramid. It provides the stability by ensuring that:

- The *mission* is sensible and attainable.
- *Objectives* are realistic.
- *Goals* fit with objectives.
- *Strategies* are innovative.

In addition, much of the benefit of strategic thinking lies in the process itself and not simply in the end result. If properly approached, employees who participate gain insights into their industry that are otherwise unobtainable. They begin to see the unique cause-effect relationship between their bank and the rest of the world. They gradually cultivate their imaginations. Ideas generate more ideas. Before long, you have a bank full of people who are thinking strategically. They are subconsciously monitoring all elements in their environment trying to determine their strategic implication.

13 PUSHING THROUGH CONSTRAINTS TO EFFECTIVE STRATEGY

"Every new opinion, at its starting, is precisely in a minority of one."

... Thomas Carlyle

Whenever management undertakes a project that requires people to change how they approach their jobs, resistance is encountered. This is especially true in the banking profession because many people entered the industry when the formula for profit was relatively straight forward due to the stability of the competitive environment.

As the CEO you must identify existing and potential sources of resistance to strategic planning and deal with them. If left unchecked, they can sabotage an otherwise successful plan. One of your primary challenges is to manage the human side of change. This involves being able to successfully address the following constraints to planning:

- Tradition
- Past failures
- Lack of time
- Unpredictability of future
- Paralysis of analysis
- Fear of commitment
- Malicious obedience
- Negative attitudes
- Incompetence of personnel
- Politics
- Fear of failure
- Bureaucracy
- Parochialism
- Lack of resources

The balance of this chapter discusses each constraint and suggests several ways to overcome them.

Tradition

"Do you remember? We second-guessed First State Bank and got those money market certificates out on the street without any strategic plan. We've always done okay before. Why do we need one now?"

The employee making this remark could be so steeped in tradition and "the way we've always done it before" that his background in traditional banking makes it hard for him to recognize the benefits of a change. Many consider tradition to be the single greatest constraint for planning in banks. Traditional thinking has prevented any meaningful consideration of threats posed by the vast array of new market entrants, such as, Sears, Penney's, American Express and others.

Our recommendation: Emphasize to the employee the need to be flexible and adapt to a constantly changing environment. Make the point that any information gathering process that helps develop meaningful knowledge regarding the bank will help business. Strategic planning can only help to enhance the bank's knowledge of internal and external situations. Armed with this information, the bank is better equipped to deal with difficult business problems.

Past Failures

"Do you recall the time we developed a three year plan for our branch in Baker? It folded within a year."

Hopefully, this employee is not attributing the branch's failure to planning. He is certainly suggesting that planning isn't synonymous with success. The problem in Baker may not have been the plan but the manner in which it was implemented. Although the plan may have been inadequate, the failure may have been far worse had there been no plan at all.

Our recommendation: Indicate that we can make future planning efforts more effective by understanding why our previous plans did not materialize. Point out other examples of failures where there were no planning efforts.

Lack of Time

"I don't have the time to spend on strategic planning. Our first

priority right now should be to change the advertising slogan on our market interest account."

This is a common human reaction from a highly motivated action-oriented bank manager. However, a fundamental premise of planning is to become more effective, even at the apparent price of near-term efficiency. It is the "doing the right things," not just "doing things right" philosophy.

Our recommendation: Tell him that good planning will serve to help him use his time more effectively. Explain that he can limit the amount of time spent on planning. Planners can and should establish and adhere to a timetable, which will serve to limit the scope of the planning process to a manageable and relevant level.

Indicate to the employee that time spent on planning should be seen as an investment in the future — his as well as the bank's. At times increasing competition, changing regulations and revised pricing structures may seem overwhelming but state that planning will help to anticipate external pressures and prepare the bank to meet them more effectively.

Unpredictability of Future

"Remember when we thought that First National Bank would not offer variable-rate mortgages for at least six months and it happened the next day? Who knows what the future could possibly bring?"

This employee would probably prefer to wait until tomorrow to see what will happen because he believes the future cannot be predicted. The attitude of this employee is understandable but does not take into account the continuing uncertainties bankers will always have to contend with.

Our recommendation: Explain that planning will force the bank to define its assumptions about the future, enabling it to anticipate rather than react to future events. Note that planning will help the bank determine its future direction. Point out that uncertainty has been true throughout history. Next year there will be a new economy, new competition, revised regulations, additional products and the like. Always stress that a strategic plan is not a static document. If there are significant changes in the business environment we can always change the plan.

Paralysis of Analysis

"We don't have enough information, enough data to do a plan. Let's wait until we have more facts and can do a little more analysis."

This attitude doesn't just crop up in large banks with extensive staff capabilities. Any bank can have difficulty getting moving because there always seems to be another analysis to be done or bit of information to consider first.

Our recommendation: Suggest that all information has a certain time value. The bank should determine a limit on the amount of time gathering data because there is a point of diminishing returns. Point out that all business decisions are made with less than complete knowledge. The fact that more reliable data is not available is no excuse for not planning; it only makes the risks of decision making greater. Be careful to recognize the contributions of those who perform the analysis. Assist them in managing their own time by setting due dates and providing leadership where analysis offers the greatest potential payback.

Fear of Commitment

"Plan? Why should I take on another responsibility? I've just taken over three new accounts and I'm not willing to run the risk that I'll do a less than top-notch job with the responsibility I already have."

This response may be due to the climate of the bank. Is the employee fearful that if his performance is less than 100% he'll be reprimanded?

Our recommendation: Determine whether this employee is aware of how performance is evaluated. Because most individuals have multiple responsibilities, management generally recognizes that all will not be discharged by the same standard.

Explain to this person that he should view planning as part of an overall integration of management responsibilities. Planning should be considered as a routine and vital part of the management process, no different from other operational functions. Explain that the new responsibilities should get easier as one gains experience.

Malicious Obedience

"If you want me to plan, I'll plan! You're the boss."

Any planning done with this kind of "I'm not convinced, but if I have to do it I will" attitude probably will be worthless. This employee will go through the motions but probably feels "why should I try, you don't care anyway."

Our recommendation: Ask yourself why someone would react this way. Is it the fault of bank management? This attitude can occur when management does not listen effectively to employees or is not genuinely open to their ideas.

Negative Attitudes

"This strategic plan is going to be a lot of work. It's not going to make any difference to the bank. People are just too busy. It will never work. I consider this project to be of no possible value."

Such a stonewall attitude of negativism is quite serious. Quite possibly whatever you say or suggest to this employee won't do much good.

Our recommendation: Seriously counsel the employee. If he is this negative about strategic planning, he is probably negative about a lot of things. Someone with such an attitude has a disruptive impact on others. If his attitude cannot be changed, you will want to isolate him to contain his attitude while he is still with the bank. The bank's best long term solution may have to involve his dismissal and replacement.

Incompetence of Personnel

"I can't even decide on making this loan. And you want me to help develop a strategic plan?"

This employee may not have the capacity or the ability to be effective in the planning effort without help.

Our recommendation: First, make certain you have selected the most qualified person for the planning job at hand. If so, consider additional training as a possible longer-term solution. In the near-term, you may wish to engage the services of a consultant to supplement areas where existing skills are deficient. Eventual replacement of personnel whose skills cannot be improved through training and counseling is absolutely essential.

Politics

"I work for Stu, but now I'm going to have to develop a long-range plan for marketing our IRA's? And report to Joe? What's in it for me? Who does my evaluation and where will my raises come from anyway?"

This employee views the planning process as an opportunity to reposition himself within the bank. He could spend much of his time and energy on the process and not the substance.

Our recommendation: Recognize and reward team players. This should give him a quick message about how to be successful in your bank. You may decide to initiate counseling or provide some guidance to this employee. The bank should be concerned about an individual who places excessive reliance on personal goals and ambitions rather than the bank's goals. Let him know if he works toward the bank goals, the personal advancement will come by itself.

Fear of Failure

"I'm afraid of setting an objective for our loan officers for selling credit life insurance because what would happen if we don't meet what amounts to a quota?"

Many bank employees fear taking a personal risk because they might not meet their objective. Their perception is that bank management will not recognize how far they have come, but rather how far they fall short of meeting a goal. This attitude also can stem from a lack of personal self-confidence.

Our recommendation: Point out that if objectives are not established, goals will not be met. However, the individual should set his own objective with the direction and encouragement of senior management. When an employee participates in setting his own objectives, he will feel more committed to the planning process.

Bureaucracy

"Let's see if I got it right. The plan should be cleared with Steve, but first I should talk to Jim and then the next step is..."

Procedures at a bank can get bogged down with excessive protocol, resulting in a lot of frustration for employees at all levels.

Our recommendation: Reward timeliness and responsiveness. Have tight time schedules if necessary to force a quick response. If the task is accomplished through channels, fine. If not, avoid asking too many questions about who cleared what with whom. In highly structured areas, develop project oriented groups and committees to participate in the decision making process of the planning effort. With fewer layers, there will be more and better communication.

Parochialism

"I don't understand why these types of corporate loans should be centralized. We are perfectly capable of servicing them adequately in this branch."

This employee is showing greater loyalty to his branch than the overall bank. His attitude of we can do it just as well as the main office is interfering with his ability to see things from a more macro perspective.

Our recommendation: Make certain you are communicating the "results" of this individual's responsibilities from the bank's overall perspective. Possibly in the longer term, placing this person on an assignment in the main office might change his perspective. Make certain that other personnel who make sacrifices in their operation for the benefit of the bank as a whole are properly recognized.

Lack of Resources

"With our limited capital base there are so few strategic choices that are possible, isn't this whole planning effort a waste of time?"

In this comment, the employee refers to a lack of financial

resources, but the "lack" could be technical competence, clerical manpower or adequate management skills.

Our recommendation: Perhaps the plan should focus on generating more resources through planning. Communicate to the bank employee that the planning process should lead to a more efficient and effective allocation of scarce resources as a result of determining how best to deploy them.

Conclusion

For effective strategic planning you must resolve the fundamental anti-planning biases or constraints. Recognize that the essence of the problem is one of resistance to change, whether subtle or not. We did not attempt in the short space of this chapter to discuss the full dimension of the human response to change. Instead our purpose was to introduce you to some of the most prevalent constraints we have observed in initiating strategic management.

To overcome the constraints to planning, one must:

- Recognize that there are a number of reasons why resistance is encountered and that most concerns have some kind of rational basis.
- Determine exactly what may produce resistance to change in the minds of your employees. You can accomplish this through an ongoing dialogue.
- Communicate clearly the purpose and value of strategic planning in order to achieve total commitment.
- Minimize the uncertainty involved in planning by listening and being genuinely open to new ideas.
- Reward the bank managers who effectively achieve planning goals and objectives.

Some psychologists suggest that the bottom line to all constraints is the fear of losing. Often, managers are not focused on winning as much as they are focused on appearing not to lose. By avoiding risk they may not be winning, but they are also not losing.

Senior management, and the CEO in particular, need to show bank employees that it is possible to function in a new way without fear and be effective. This requires the CEO to become a model for working with change and to provide leadership that facilitates an experience of winning.

14 GOING BEYOND

"Our aspirations are our possibilities."
... Robert Browning

Finally we want to say that, despite economic conditions and competitive threats, we believe that banks will make it. They will persist but not without some significant restructuring and the good solid foundation of effective strategic management.

This monograph really has been about how to constructively manage change. Bankers have choices to make about how they will react to an environment where the regulatory climate, work place, economy and competition are always changing. They can choose to be the cause of change or the effect of it. Those who choose to be at the effect will always be reacting to external conditions. By your choosing to be the cause or at the cause of change, you will be fully participating in creating an environment that insures your bank's future success.

We are confident that the suggestions and techniques given in this monograph work. They help to form a basis and springboard not only to deal with short-term problems but also to get a handle on long-term issues in the banking industry. We know it works because we have helped banks such as yours effectively create and implement a strategic plan that works.

Approach strategic planning, implementation and thinking as a creative process. Recognize that any worthwhile project is not easy but your efforts will pay off.

We encourage you not to be afraid to expect excellence and top-notch performance from your staff. Also expect that there will be for you and your employees emotional peaks and valleys associated with the frustration of directing strategy changes in the bank.

Keeping all this in mind, we know that you can develop a synergistic esprit de corps within the bank, that encourages less protection of old traditional methods and more open, flexible and progressive thinking. As you help create a positive, can-do climate within the bank, you will enable your institution to move to new levels of success.

When most people discuss strategic planning, they speak specifically of formulating business strategy and about continuing implementation efforts. We have considered these topics. However, we are not simply concerned with strategic planning, but rather, strategic management.

In order to become strategic managers, one must develop an organization in the bank that will support strategic management. You must seek the extra ingredient that converts key operating people into strategic thinkers. When this is accomplished, the term *strategic management* will be taken for granted as the pervasive method of operation.

APPENDIX

and

BIBLIOGRAPHY

APPENDIX

INDEXES[1]

Ayer Directory of Publications, Bala Cynwyd, PA: Ayer Press, annual.

Published annually. List U.S., U.S. territory and Canadian newspapers, magazines and trade publications. Covers consumer, business, technical, professional and trade publications.

Bibliographic Guide to Business and Economics. Boston: G.K. Hall & Co.

A comprehensive bibliography of books by topic, title, and author. Published annually.

Brownstone, David and Carruth, Corton, *Where to Find Business Information.* New York: John Wiley & Sons, 1979.

A listing of a wide variety of publications indexed by subject, publisher and source of business information.

Daniells, Lorna. *Business Information Sources.* Berkley: University of California Press, 1976.

Excellent bibliography arranged by subject.

Directory of Information Resources in the U.S. National Referral Center for Science and Technology, Vol. I-IV.

Two volumes are of interest: "Federal Government" and "Social Sciences."

Wasserman, Paul, ed. *Encyclopedia of Business Information Sources.* Vol. I and II. Detroit: Gale Research Co., 1970.

An excellent resource that references articles, books and pamphlets. Information organized alphabetically and geographically.

Wasserman, Paul, ed. *Statistics Sources.* Detroit: Gale Research Co., 1982.

A subject guide to data on industrial, business, social, educational, financial and other topics for the U.S. and Internationally.

GENERAL BUSINESS AND BANKING[2]

Magazines, Newsletters and Newspapers

American Banker, New York: American Banker, Inc.

Daily newspaper covering news related to banking, including

[1]Bibliographical descriptions adapted from Daniells, *Business Information Sources* and Brownstone and Carruth, *Where to Find Business Information.*

[2]Bibliographical descriptions from Brownstone & Carruth's *Where to Find Business Information.*

legislation, mergers, money markets, and international developments.

Andrews Newsletter. Valencia, CA: R.E. Andrews and Associates. Looseleaf, monthly.

Investment advisory service based primarily on technical analysis of market activity.

Bank Automation Newsletter. Boston: Warren, Gorham & Lamont, Inc.

Monthly newsletter. Reports on bank and electronic data processing services and products including electronic funds and transfer systems.

Bank Card Newsletter. American Bankers Association.

Monthly newsletter covering bank credit card field. Sends subscribers mailings on American Bankers Association, Bank Card Division, conferences, workshops, schools and statistical surveys.

Bank Installation Lending Newsletter. Boston: Warren Gorham, & Lamont, Inc., Pamphlet, monthly.

News and commentary on trends and developments in bank installment lending.

Bank Marketing. Chicago: Bank Marketing Association.

Short articles on advertising, marketing and public relations of interest to bank managers. Published monthly.

Banker. London: Financial Times Ltd.

Articles on banking and monetary policy of worldwide interest.

Bankers Magazine. Boston: Warren, Gorham & Lamont, Inc.

Bi-monthly magazine. Discusses bank planning, operations, controls and management.

Bankers Monthly. Northbrook, IL: Bankers Monthly, Inc.

A national trade magazine for banking and investments.

Banking. New York: Simmons-Boardman Publishing Corporation. Monthly journal of the American Bankers Association. Articles on bank management and long-range planning for commercial banks and trust companies.

Barclays Review. London: Barclays Bank

Quarterly bank letters that analyze current financial and economic trends.

Burroughs Clearing House. Detroit: Burroughs Corporation.

Trade journal of the financial services industry. Published monthly.

Business Week. New York: McGraw-Hill, weekly.

Reports on U.S. and international business and economic topics.

Conference Board Record. New York: the Conference Board, monthly.

Reports on Conference Board research projects and developments in business and economics.

Federal Home Loan Bank Board Journal, Washington, D.C.: U.S. Government Printing Office, monthly.

Discusses housing and home finance issues. Reports on the activities and policies of the U.S. Federal Home Loan Bank Board. Provides mortgage, housing, and general financial data.

Federal Reserve Bulletin, Washington D.C.: U.S. Board of Governors of the Federal Reserve System, annual.

Single best source for current U.S. banking and monetary statistics.

Financial Executive. New York: Financial Executives Institute.

Monthly magazine that covers new developments and offers practical information in the field of corporate finance.

Financial World. New York: Macro Communities.

A weekly analysis of general investment situations, prospects for industries and individual companies.

Harvard Business Review. Boston: Graduate School of Business Administration, Harvard University.

Bimonthly review. Provides an analysis of conditions and problems in all business areas.

Institutional Investor. New York: Institutional Investor Systems, Inc.

A monthly journal with articles on corporate financing, pension fund management, investor relations, profiles of specific managers.

Journal of Bank Research. Park Ridge, IL: Bank Administration Institute.

Quarterly magazine. Covers application of new ideas in science and technology to banking practice.

Journal of Finance. New York: American Finance Association, Graduate School of Business Administration, New York University. Technical articles on all phases of finance.

Journal of Management Studies. Oxford, England: Basil Blackwell & Mott Ltd.

Scholarly articles of management theory, advertising, financial institutions, personnel studies and marketing written primarily by British educators and researchers.

Journal of Money, Credit & Banking. Columbus, Ohio: Ohio State University Press.

Research studies by professors and economists.

Leaders Letter. American Institute of Banking.

Newsletter that reports on American Institute of Banking's chapter activities and programs.

Magazine of Bank Administration. Park Ridge, IL: Bank Administration Institute.

Published monthly. Practical articles on accounting, administration, bank building and organization, credit cards, automation, payment systems, bank security, personnel and taxes.

Managerial Planning. Oxford, OH: Planning Executives Institute.

Bimonthly magazine. Articles on budgeting, profit planning and corporate planning.

Marketing Economics Guide. New York: Marketing Economic Institute, annual.

Gives information to assist in developing effective marketing strategy.

Money Manager. New York. Bond Buyer.

Weekly newspaper. Especially useful for its news and statistical coverage on mortgage, corporate, international, and U.S. financial market.

Payment Systems Newsletter. New York: Payment Systems, Inc. Pamphlet, monthly.

Developments in bank payment systems and electronic fund transfers.

Savings Bank Journal. New York: National Association of Mutual Savings Banks.

Monthly magazine. Trends in savings banking field.

REPORTS, DIRECTORIES, BOOKS

Acquisition Newsletter International. New York: Newsletters, Inc.

News of international corporate acquisition activity and listings of companies available for acquisition or seeking to acquire other firms.

Almanac of Business and Industrial Financial Ratios. Englewood Cliffs, NJ: Prentice-Hall, Inc.

Financial and operating ratios for about 160 industries including banks and financial industries, as well as the usual manufacturing, wholesaling, retailing industries.

America's Fastest Growing Companies. Greenwich, CT: John S. Harold, Inc.

Monthly publication. An information service devoted to identifying and monitoring the progress of approximately 150 publicly owned companies judged to have the fastest growth in new income per share.

BHC Report. Rockville Centre, NY: Paul Kagan Associates, Inc.

Semi-monthly publication. News and commentary on financial and investment issues affecting bank holding companies.

Business Failure Record. New York: Dun & Bradstreet.

Statistics on business failures, issued weekly, monthly and quarterly.

Directory of Business and Financial Services. 7th edition. New York: Special Libraries Association.

This is the latest edition of an excellent directory that describes business, economic and financial services. Published periodically with regular supplements.

Directory of Corporate Affiliations: Who Owns Whom. Skokie, IL: National Register Publishing Co., Inc.

Identifies parent companies, their divisions, subsidiaries, and affiliates of the major corporations in the United States.

Federal Banking Law Reports. Chicago: Commercial Clearing House.

Federal banking controls as reflected by The Federal Reserve System, the National Banking Acts, deposit insurance, monetary regulations, and the federal lending agencies.

Finance Facts Yearbook. Washington: National Consumer Finance Association.

Brief text, with statistics and charts, on consumers - their income, spending, finance and credit management, as well as the consumer installment credit industry.

Glen G. Munn's Encyclopedia of Banking and Finance, 7th edition. Boston. Bankers Publishing Co.

The latest edition of an excellent one-volume encyclopedia covering the whole area of banking and finance.

Intelligence Digest, Business Trends. Gloucestershire, England: Intelligence.

Monthly newsletter, Political strategy and economic review of world affairs.

Million Dollar Directory, New York: Dun & Bradstreet.

Lists approximately 39,000 U.S. companies with an indicated worth of $1 million or more.

Moody's Bank and Finance Manual. New York: Moody's Investors Service.

Information about each company includes a brief corporate history; a list of subsidiaries, principal plants and properties; business and products; officers and directors; comparative income statements, balance sheet statistics, selected financial ratios; description of outstanding securities.

Mortgage Banking: Financial Statements and Operating Ratios. Washington: Mortgage Bankers Assn. of America.

Operating ratios and balance sheet statistics, based on the experience of over 200 mortgage banking companies.

National Fact Book of Mutual Savings Banks. New York: National Association of Mutual Savings Banks.

Statistics that cover the structure and operations of the savings bank industry and its role in savings and mortgage markets.

Polk's World Bank Directory Supplement Service. Nashville, TN: R.L. Polk & Co. Pamphlet.

Reports on new banks, new branches, mergers, closures, and changes of address for banks in Canada and U.S.

Poor's Register of Corporations, Directors and Executives. New York: Standard & Poor's Corporation.

Directory of about 34,000 public and privately owned corporations and their directors and officers.

Savings and Loan Fact Book. Chicago: U.S. League of Saving Associations, annual.

Brief text with statistics and charts on savings, home ownership, residential construction and financing; also data on the savings and loan business and on related federal government agencies.

Savings and Loan Investor. Long Beach, CA: Savings and Loan Investor.

News and investment advice about savings and loan stocks.

Venture Capital. Chicago: S.M. Rubel & Co.

News and statistics on small business investment companies and other corporate investors of venture capital as well as on companies funded by venture capital.

Washington Banktrends. Wayne, NJ: Washington Banktrends, Kennedy Sinclaire Inc.

News of economic, financial, and political developments affecting banks, savings and loan associations, credit unions, and other financial institutions.

Who's Who in Finance and Industry. Chicago: Marquis Publications.

Career sketches of leading businessmen and others noteworthy in the fields of finance and industry.

SERVICES

Annual Statement Studies. Philadelphia, PA: Robert Morris Associates.

This contains financial and operating ratios for about 300 lines of business - manufacturers, wholesalers, services and contractors - based on information obtained from member banks of RMA.

Consensus of Insiders. Fort Lauderdale, FL: Consensus of Insiders.

Investment advisory service based on analysis of stock transactions of stock exchange members, specialists, and traders; corporate insiders; and mutual and pension funds. Includes advice on market timing based on indices of risk exposure and actions of market professionals, and a commentary on patterns in insider trading.

Predicasts. Cleveland, OH: Predicasts, Inc.

This useful quarterly service gives short and long range forecast statistics both for basic economic indicators and for individual products (by SIC number).

U.S. Bureau of the Census. Washington: G.P.O.

Reports on population, housing, manufacturers, selected services, construction, retail trade, wholesale trade, and enterprise statistics.

Value Line Investment Survey. New York: Arnold Bernhard & Co.

Investment advisory service offering detailed background information and investment evaluations on over 1,500 common stocks, including nearly all issues listed in the New York Stock Exchange.

BANK LETTERS

Business in Brief. New York: Chase Manhattan Bank, bimonthly. Highlights economic trends of interest to bankers.

ECONOMIC INFORMATION[3]

Publications

Assets, Liabilities and Capital Accounts, Commercial and Mutual Savings Banks, also known as "FDIC Reports of Call," published quarterly by the FDIC, available through the Federal Reserve Research Department for all state and national banks.

Banking Law Journal. Boston: Warren, Gorham & Lamont, monthly.

Covers banking law developments and includes digests of cases and book reviews.

Census of Business, every five years and *County Business Patterns,* annually, U.S. Department of Commerce, Bureau of Census.

The Conference Board Record, New York: The Conference Board.

Monthly commentary and analysis of trends in business and economics.

Dodge Construction Statistics. New York: F.W. Dodge Division, McGraw-Hill Information Systems Co., monthly.

Two separate publications that give statistics on construction contract awards: (1) a 3-section "United States Summary Bulletin: and (2) a more detailed "Region Bulletin" available for all 9 regions of the U.S.

Economic Statistics Bureau of Washington, D.C., *Handbook of Basic Economic Statistics,* annual, with monthly supplements.

Current and historical statistics on industry, commerce, labor and agriculture.

Federal Banking Law Reports. Chicago: Commerce Clearing House, weekly publication.

Reports on the Federal Reserve System, deposit insurance, national bank acts and related federal banking and loan measures.

International Financial Statistics, International Monetary Fund, monthly.

Gives statistics on domestic and international finance including exchange rates, international liquidity and government finance.

---

[3]Bibliographical descriptions from Daniells, *Business Information Sources* and Brownstone and Carruth, *Where to Find Business Information.*

Issues in Bank Regulations. The Bank Administration Institute, magazine published quarterly.

Articles and news items on proposed and existing bank regulations. Includes views of bankers and bank regulators in discussions of regulatory issues.

Marketing Economics Guide. New York: Marketing Economics Institute, annual.

Provides information to help develop effective marketing strategy.

Monthly Economic Letter, New York: Citibank.

Provides a current summary of economic and financial conditions and trends. Includes quarterly net income figures of leading corporations, by industry groups.

Municipal Yearbook. Washington, D.C.: International City Management Association.

Covers developments in U.S. and Canadian municipal government.

Sales and Marketing Management, "Survey of Buying Power," New York.

Marketing and economic researchers usually turn to this important issue first when they seek current estimates showing U.S. and Canadian geographic variations in population, income and retail business.

Statistical Yearbook. New York: United Nations, annual.

Provides data on world population, production, trade, consumption and public finance.

Survey of Current Business, U.S. Department of Commerce, monthly.

Reports on U.S. economic conditions, specifically corporate profits, gross national product, employment, plant and equipment expenditures, and U.S. international transactions.

U.S. Bureau of the Census, *Statistical Abstract of the United States, Washington, D.C.: U.S. Government Printing Office, annual.*

Prime source for U.S. industrial, social, political and economic statistics and serves as a bibliographical guide.

U.S. Council of Economic Advisors, *Economic Indicators,* Washington, D.C.: U.S. Government Printing Office, annual report.

Statistical tables and charts for the basic economic indicators.

U.S. Department of Commerce: *Survey of Business* from Office of Business Economics; *Business Conditions Digest* from Bureau of Economic Analysis; *Survey of Manufacturers,* etc. from Bureau of Census; *United States Industrial Outlook* from Business and Defense Service Administration; "Guide to Foreign Trade Statistics" from Bureau of Census; "Overseas Business Reports" and "Foreign Economic Trends and Their Implications for the U.S." from the Bureau of Inter-National Commerce; Bureau of Census, *Census of Population,* every decade; *Current Population Reports,* irregular; *Statistical Abstract of the United States,* annually; and *County and City Data Book,* irregularly.

U.S. Department of Housing and Urban Development, *Housing and Urban Development Trends,* quarterly.

Provides current statistics on housing production and financing as well as the programs of HUD.

U.S. Office of Management and Budget, *Social Indicators.* Executive Office of the President, Washington, D.C.: U.S. Government Printing Office.

Selected statistics and charts on U.S. social conditions and trends, covering health, public safety, education, employment, income, housing, leisure, recreation, and population.

Washington Financial Reports. Bureau of National Affairs, published weekly.

Reports on federal developments affecting banks, savings and loan associations, holding companies and credit unions.

Yearbook of Labor Statistics, O.I.T., International Labor Office.

Summarizes labor statistics in 190 countries in areas such as population, employment, wages, productivity and hours worked.

COMPETITIVE ENVIRONMENT INFORMATION

Publications

Area banking data published by the 12 regional Federal Reserve Banks, availability varies by region; examples: *Bank Debits,* monthly; *Commercial Loans by Industry,* weekly; *Functional Cost Analysis,* annual; *Municipal Obligations,* semiannual; *Operating Statistics,* annual; *Time and Savings Deposit Survey,* quarterly; and *Weekly Report of Condition.*

Bank Operating Statistics, Federal Deposit Insurance Corp., annual.

Statistics on accounts and deposits for commercial banks and mutual savings banks.

Gunther, E. and Goldstein, F.A., *Current Sources of Marketing Information.* (American Marketing Association Bibliography Series No. 6) Chicago: American Marketing Assn., 1960.

Provides an annotated list arranged by subject of books, government reports and special studies published since 1954. It also includes a section on periodicals.

Market Guide. New York: Editor & Publisher.

Individual market survey of over 1,500 U.S. and Canadian cities. Data includes population, location, trade area, banks, principle industries, colleges and universities, department and chain stores, newspapers, retail outlets, and sales.

Monthly Report on Deposit Flows at Savings and Loan Associations, Federal Home Loan Banks.

Moody's Bank and Finance Manual. New York: Moody's Investors Service, annual, with semi-weekly supplements.

Brief histories of each bank, officers, and directors including comparative financial statement and stock price activity.

Report of Condition and Report of Income and Dividends, Federal Deposit Insurance Corp.

Information on individual banks.

Sheshunoff.

Banks of individual states, growth and market share analysis, complete market share report and financial analysis.

Statistics of Continents: Source of Market Research.

Includes separate books on *Africa, America, Europe.*

U.S. Bureau of the Census, Statistical Abstract of the U.S. Washington: G.P.O.

Prime source for U.S. industrial, social, political and economic statistics.

Yearbook of International Trade Statistics, United Nations.

Gives a compilation of trade statistics.

Yearbook of National Accounts Statistics, United Nations.

Provides national income, gross national product, and other national statistics by country over a 12-year period.

GOVERNMENTAL AND REGULATORY INFORMATION[4]

Publications

Applied Science and Technology Index. Bronx, NY: H.W. Wilson Co.

Monthly index that covers articles published in a wide range of scientific and technological journals.

Bank Officer's Handbook of Commercial Banking Law. Boston: Warren, Gorham & Lamont, 4th Edition, 1974.

Nontechnical coverage of ordinary legal problems within the bank.

Code of Federal Regulation. Washington: National Archives & Record Service.

Codification of the general and permanent rules published in the Federal Register by the Executive departments and agencies of the Federal government.

Economic Report of the President. Washington: U.S. Council of Economic Advisors.

Annual book. A publication of the economic report of the U.S. President transmitted to Congress and the report of the Council of Economic Advisors. Includes information on the world economy and statistical tables.

Federal Register. Washington: Office of the Federal Register.

Gives a uniform system for making available the public regulations and legal notices issued by Federal agencies.

Kiplinger Washington Newsletter. Weekly.

Provides briefings on business trends and includes pertinent government policies and information on employment, investment, and interest rates.

Monthly Catalog of United States Government Publications. Superintendent of Documents, G.P.O.

Monthly list of recently issued government publications.

Public Affairs Information Services Bulletin. New York: Public Affairs Information Service, Inc.

Weekly bulletin that contains a list of books, publications, and articles relating to economic and social conditions, public administration and international relations.

---

[4]Bibliographical descriptions from Brown and Carruth's *Where to Find Business Information.*

U.S. Bureau of the Census. *Statistical Abstract of the United States.* Washington: G.P.O.

Prime source for U.S. industrial, social, political and economic statistics.

U.S. Department of Labor: *Producer Prices and Price Indexes* monthly; *Handbook of Labor Statistics.*

The Handbook is an annual report from the Bureau of Labor Statistics.

U.S. Department of the Treasury: *Treasury Bulletin.* Washington: G.P.O.

Monthly report containing financial and statistical tables related to federal fiscal operation.

TECHNICAL MATERIAL

CIS Index. Washington, D.C.: Congressional Information Index.

Provides a monthly abstract for all the publications of Congress. It consists of a summary section that abstracts several types of congressional reports and documents and includes an Index section that provides subjects and names of individuals and organizations.

Code of Federal Regulation. Washington: National Archives and Record Service.

Final listing of regulations.

Master Key Index. New York: Business International Corp.

Regulations, tarriffs.

BANK TECHNOLOGY

Publications

Auerback Computer Technology Reports on Financial Systems. Pennsauken, N.J.: Auerback Publishers, Inc.

Reports on computer technology.

Bank Systems and Equipment. New York: Gralla Publications.

Monthly magazine covering operations and systems management in the banking field. Focus on computer systems.

EDP Industry Report. Waltham, MA: James Peacock.

Reports on electronic data processing.

Research and Development Directory. Washington: Government Data Publications.

Annual book. Reports on government research and development contracts awarded in the past year. Indicates the awardee, agency and nature of work.

EXTERNAL DATABASES

AICPA-MAARS, Mead Data

Full text of 4,000 annual reports.

Arnold Bernhard & Co.-Value Line, ADP Network Services, Inc., Compuserve, Inc., G.E.I.S.C., Interactive Data Corp., Tymshare, Inc.

Contains financial data on 250 publicly held banks and bank holding companies that have been compiled from annual reports.

Data Courier, Inc.-ABI/Inform, Dialog.

Abstracts over 500 journals in business management and administration.

Disclosure, Inc.-Disclosure; DISCLO, Dow Jones, Mead Data, Dialog.

Contains information from the more than 11,000 publicly owned companies that file reports with the Securities and Exchange Commission.

Dun & Bradstreet, Inc. - DunSprint, Dun & Bradstreet.

Contains information from over 4 million Dun & Bradstreet business information reports on companies in the U.S.

European - American Bank and Trust Company - Eurabank, The Service Bureau Comp.

A database system containing financial information taken from the annual reports of over 1,000 banks in 72 countries in Europe, South America, North America and Australia.

Federal Deposit Insurance Corporation - FDIC, Bankcall 11, ADP Network Services, Inc., Compuserve, Inc., Interactive Data Corporation, Warner Computer Systems, Inc.

Contains data from the consolidated report of condition and income filed by all FDIC-insured commercial banks.

Federal Deposit Insurance Corporation-Financial Institution Database, The Service Bureau Comp.

Contains over 400 series of statistics on the sources and uses of funds in the U.S. economy for 50 major sectors.

Federal Home Loan Bank Board-Savings and Loan; FSLIC, ADP Network Services, Inc., Interactive Data Corporation, Timesharing Resources, Inc.

Contains data on over 4,000 federally chartered savings and loan institutions insured by the Federal Home Loan Bank Board.

Federal Home Loan Bank Board-Scan, Remote Computing Corp.

A database system that contains data from semi-annual reports submitted to the FHLBB by more than 4,000 member savings and loan associations.

Information Bank, Direct or Mead Data, N.Y. Times.

Abstracts of 10 other papers, 49 journals from 1969.

National Newspaper Index, Dialog, Christian Science Monitor, N.Y. Times, Wall Street Journal, monthly update.

Robinson-Humphrey Comp.-Bankanal, The Service Bureau Comp.

A database system containing financial information on approximately 195 of the top bank holding companies in the U.S.

BIBLIOGRAPHY

American Bankers Association, "Bank Strategic Planning: A Guide for Organizing and Managing the Process."

Arthur Andersen & Co. and Bank Administration Institute. "New Dimensions in Banking: Managing the Strategic Position" (1983).

Bank Administration Institute, "Bank Analysis from External Sources (1980).

Bank Administration Institute, "Successful Profit Planning for Banks" (1970).

Bibeault, Donald B., *Corporate Turnaround,* McGraw-Hill, Inc. (1982).

Brandt, Steven C., *Strategic Planning in Emerging Companies,* Addison-Wesley Publishing Company (1981).

Eisenberg, Joseph, *Turnaround Management,* McGraw-Hill, Inc. (1972).

Ewing, David W., *Long-Range Planning for Management,* Harper & Row (1972).

Higgins, James, *Organizational Policy and Strategic Management,* Dryden Press, 2nd edition (1983).

Kibel, H. Ronald, *How to Turn Around a Financially Troubled Company,* McGraw-Hill, Inc. (1982).

Kudla, R. J., "Elements of Effective Corporate Planning," *Long Range Planning* (August, 1976).

Lorange, Peter, *Implementation of Strategic Planning,* Prentice-Hall, Inc. (1979).

Lorange, Peter, and Vancil, Richard F., *Strategic Planning Systems,* Prentice-Hall (1977).

Lorange, Peter, and Vancil, Richard F., "How to Design a Strategic Planning System," *Harvard Business Review* (September/October 1976).

Metzger, Robert O. and Rau, Susan E., "Strategic Planning for Future Bank Growth," *The Bankers Magazine* (July-August 1982).

Naisbitt, John, *Megatrends,* Warner Book, Inc. (1982).

Naylor, Thomas H., *Strategic Planning Management,* Planning Executives Institute, Oxford, Ohio (1980).

Parker, George G. C., "Now Management Will Make or Break the Bank," *Harvard Business Review* (November-December 1981).

Pearce, John A., and Robinson, Richard B., *Strategic Management,* Richard D. Irwin, Inc. (1982).

Peters, Thomas J. and Waterman, Robert H. Jr., *In Search of Excellence,* Harper & Row Publishers, Inc. (1982).

Pezzullo, Mary Ann, *Marketing for Bankers,* American Bankers Association, Washington, D.C. (1982).

Porter, Michael E., *Competitive Strategy,* The Free Press (1980).

Quinn, James Brian, *Strategies for Change,* Richard D. Irwin, Inc. (1980).

Rothschild, William E., *Strategic Alternatives,* American Management Association, New York (1979).

Sapp, R. W. and Seiler, R.E., "The Relationship Between Long-Range Planning and Financial Performance of U.S. Commercial Banks," *Managerial Planning* (September/October 1981).

Simmons, W. W., *So You Want to Have a Long-Range Plan,* Planning Executives Institute, Oxford, Ohio (1978).

Steiner, George A., *Strategic Planning,* The Free Press (1979).

Tourangeau, Kevin W., *Strategic Management,* McGraw-Hill, Inc. (1981).